Time Hacks

Time Hacks

The Psychology of Time and How to Use It

Dr Ian Taylor

PIATKUS

PIATKUS

First published in Great Britain in 2025 by Piatkus

1 3 5 7 9 10 8 6 4 2

A CIP catalogue record for this book
is available from the British Library.

ISBN 978-034944-021-7

Printed and bound in Great Britain by
Clays Ltd, Elcograf S.p.A.

Papers used by Piatkus are from well-managed forests
and other responsible sources.

Piatkus
An imprint of
Little, Brown Book Group
Carmelite House
50 Victoria Embankment
London EC4Y 0DZ

The authorised representative
in the EEA is
Hachette Ireland
8 Castlecourt Centre
Dublin 15, D15 XTP3, Ireland
(email: info@hbgi.ie)

An Hachette UK Company
www.hachette.co.uk

Contents

1

A(nother) brief history of time

'For tribal man, space was the uncontrollable mystery. For technological man it is time that occupies the same role.'

– Marshall McLuhan, philosopher and
forecaster of the world wide web

The acclaimed 1950s novel *The Talented Mr Ripley* follows a young charlatan named Tom Ripley trying to succeed in New York, either by fair means or foul. Through a series of events, Ripley ends up in high-society Italy, adopting the role of someone who is always around but rarely noticed in any meaningful way. His acquaintances know little about his underlying motives or character, but don't seem to care. He is often disrespected by his associates, but he goes on to wreak havoc in their lives without any of them knowing the culprit. This description of Ripley is remarkably like a description of *time*. Time is always around but rarely noticed in any meaningful way. We know little about time's underlying motives or character, but don't seem to care. We frequently disrespect time, but it goes on to wreak havoc in our lives without any of us knowing the culprit.

If you were asked what time is, what would you say? It's unlikely that you would draw parallels with a fictional fraudster, but you might point to a watch, a clock or the bottom right corner of your computer screen. But these instruments are simply modern-day gadgets that report what time *it* is, they do not explain what *time* is. Stephen Hawking's cosmological classic *A Brief History of Time* eloquently and comprehensively captured time's role in the structure of the universe. From this viewpoint, a physicist might define time as the progression of events from the past to the present, and into the future. Time is viewed as existing independently of the human mind, and can be described using mathematical formulae. But even some physicists are beginning to question this definition of time. Prominent theories that attempt to unify Einstein's theory of general relativity and quantum mechanics no longer consider time as a fundamental component of the universe.

Defining time becomes even more complex when we adopt a philosophical perspective. Do the past and future exist anywhere but in the human mind? If the future does not exist yet, then how can time be a *physical* structure? The Greek philosopher Aristotle asked whether time exists at all if it consists of something that has not happened and something that isn't happening anymore. This idea of the insignificance of time is difficult for many physicists to swallow, but not for some theorists who believe that time is comparable to religion because it is nothing more than a product of human intellect and our ongoing attempts to understand the universe.

These interpretations illustrate that time is inseparable from human experience and the environment in which we live. Yet apart from a few scientists scratching their heads, the rest of us do not consider time in any detail. Time is familiar to all, but few truly understand it. The debates within physics and philosophy highlight how complicated time is. It is these complexities that arguably make us stick our heads in the sand and ignore the immense influence that time has on our thoughts, feelings and the thousands of daily decisions that we make. This relationship we have with time is the underpinning theme of this book. A healthy relationship, where we interact with time positively and use it wisely, can provide multiple benefits for our physical and mental health, as well as helping us to develop and thrive. Unfortunately, for many of us, our attitudes to and interactions with time destroy our mojos. This totally unscientific term is used throughout this book, because it perfectly sums up the characteristics and consequences of a harmonious relationship with time. This book does not aim to make you a productive super machine that has the fitness regime of a Navy Seal and the work ethic of Elon Musk. There are many other books and podcasts that aim to do that. Neither does this book aim to cure mental illness, because for that, you need professional help. 'Mojo' primarily refers to a state of harmony between different aspects of your life. This book is about achieving personally meaningful goals, maintaining healthy habits and making positive lifestyle changes, while living in line with your core values and boosting your mental and physical health. It's about knowing when to shift gears into overdrive or step off the hamster wheel of life and nourish the soul. Our relationship with time is the essential ingredient when it comes to restoring our mojos and allowing all parts of our life to function optimally.

The relationship has soured

Despite the intensity of the bond between time and the human mind, we catastrophically fail to recognise that the relationship has turned sour. Ironically, most of us do not have time to understand time. Numerous surveys in developed countries demonstrate that levels of boredom[1] and busyness[2] are simultaneously rife. We are seemingly trapped between monotony and mania. Consequently, many despise time for its ability to disappear when we need it, or for its abundance when we do not. Occasional bouts of boredom and busyness are innocuous, nothing more than a minor irritation in your day. But sustained boredom is implicated in the early stages of depression, overeating, excessive consumption of alcohol and self-harm.[3, 4, 5, 6] On the other hand, prolonged time pressures are associated with sleep problems, headaches, digestive problems and poor mental health.[7, 8, 9] Time is causing us significant harm, but we are doing very little about it.

The relationship with time has become so distorted in some individuals that they are, literally, terrified of time. Chronophobia is a specific disorder concerning the fear of time progressing. Individuals with this disorder irrationally and uncontrollably believe that time is passing them by, and they are wasting it by achieving nothing. People suffering with chronophobia often have cripplingly low self-esteem and high anxiety.[10] In the past, this disorder was often called 'prison neurosis', because it was largely reserved for inmates. Similar conditions, such as gerascophobia (the pathological fear of growing old) and thanatophobia (the excessive fear of dying), are observed in the elderly and the terminally ill. But then the

Covid-19 pandemic gripped the world in 2020. Sufferers of pandemic-induced chronophobia feared time slipping away during quarantine and lockdowns. They lived by the clock, wondering when the isolation would end, and attempted to cope in various ill-advised ways, like using alcohol and drugs. Chrono- and Corona-based fear in perfect destructive harmony. Most of the major implications of the pandemic have passed, yet those afflicted with chronophobia still suffer flashbacks.

While the diagnosis of this disorder is rare, many more individuals experienced the depressing feeling that they were 'wasting time' during the pandemic and were helpless to prevent it. These stolen years meant missing out on time with loved ones, significant gaps in education, or just missing out on living life to its fullest. Prior to the pandemic, approximately eight per cent of US adults experienced anxiety symptoms, and six per cent experienced symptoms of depression. During the pandemic, these figures rocketed to approximately thirty per cent for both conditions.[11] Even those who evaded mental illness were very likely to have experienced a weird distortion of time. During the lockdowns, a day seemed like a week for some, time rushed by for others, and the rest of us experienced a mindboggling mix of the two.[12]

The pandemic might be an extreme scenario, but other illustrations of time influencing our mojos are everywhere. Many of our concerns – from daily worries to existential crises – stem from our relationship with time. Am I wasting my time in this meeting? Why don't I have any free time? Am I going to be on time? Can I manage my time better? Is this the right time to look for a better job/have a relationship/buy a house? Am I making the best use of my time on Earth? The adverse effect of time on deteriorating levels of mental and physical health demonstrates how dysfunctional our relationship with time has become. This state of disrepair was not always the case.

Where did it go wrong?

Any subject worth writing about should have an ancient god associated with it. The ancient Greeks had at least three gods of time; the most celebrated was Chronos. Greek mythology has become somewhat distorted and confused over time. In early writings, Chronos was distinct from Cronus, who memorably cut off his father's genitals and ate his children (and a rock that he thought was his son, Zeus). The two gods eventually merged, helped by the ancient Romans, who blended the characteristics of the two Greek deities into their equivalent, Saturn. Most art and literature subsequently depicted Chronos as a bearded old man holding a scythe and an hourglass, resembling Death. The Hindu goddess of time, Kali, is often pictured dancing on corpses, wearing a belt of skulls and severed hands. These portrayals illustrate some of our earliest beliefs about time. Time was all powerful. Time was worshipped.

Our relationship with time evolved when we began to measure it. The ancient Egyptians developed sundials and similar instruments to measure time around 1500 BCE, and these devices remained common for over three millennia. Cleopatra and her forebears split daylight periods into twelve sections, which formed the basis for modern twelve- and twenty-four-hour timekeeping. Of course, a major flaw in this technique was that the periods varied according to the seasons and location. The further away one was from the equator, the more the twelve periods varied. In the northernmost parts of the Egyptian empire (modern-day Syria), daylight varied by approximately four hours over the course of a year. As the use of the twelve periods spread across the globe, this variation became even more dramatic. Another feature of this timekeeping system was that time stopped during the night because human activity stopped. This oddity may seem unthinkable now, but what is the point of measuring something that isn't useful? Our ancestors did not think of time as we do now. Time was flexible.

Living life according to the sun seems idyllic. Start the day when the sun rises, retire to bed when it sets. But what if it is cloudy? More importantly, as global societies developed, people began to desire consistency. In Europe, during the Middle Ages, sandglasses (a precursor to the hourglass, originally made from two bottles with their openings attached) and candles began to be used as continuous measures of time without needing to keep an eye on the sun. The widespread uptake of devices like these provided the illusion that time unfurls predictably and reliably forward. This impression was mirrored in folklore and literature. For example, a derivative of the phrase 'time and tide wait for no man' appeared in 1395 in Geoffrey Chaucer's prologue to the Clerk's Tale. A marked change in how we viewed time became apparent, and it was during this period that the first cracks in our relationship with time were seen. We no longer benefited from time aligning with the seasons and the sun, and we began to attempt to control something that was once worshipped. Time was now consistent. Time was now unrelenting.

Increased ability to travel further altered our relationship
with time. In the nineteenth century, the railway networks of
industrialised countries were chaotic because the time showing on one city's clock would often differ to that in another
city by several minutes. At one point in the United States, over
eighty regional timetables were used, each based on their own
local time. The increasing reliance on rail meant a uniform
timetable became necessary. English rail companies decided
to run their timetables according to the time in London.
Despite some local resistance, almost all public clocks in
England began to show London time by 1855, which would
later become known as Greenwich Mean Time, or GMT.
Because of the United Kingdom's global influence and ship-
ping prowess, GMT became the standard by which all other
times were calibrated across the world (the last country to
adopt standardised time zones benchmarked by GMT was
Nepal, as recently as 1986). The Greenwich Observatory
knew that they held precious information, and would charge
a fee for clients to receive the precise time via telegraph lines.
Time became a commodity. Viewing something so fundamental to our existence in this way leads to damaging individual
and societal consequences. Just look at what is unfolding
around the world thanks to our similar attempts to treat natural resources as a commodity.

Viewing time as a purchasable and consistent product
cemented artificial views on time into our psyche, but every
now and again we are forced to acknowledge this mistake.
On twenty-six occasions in the last fifty years, a second has
been added to everyone's day to adjust for the Earth wobbling
and the rate of its spin changing. For instance, when El Niño,
a climatic system in the Pacific, causes wind speed to change

dramatically, it can slow the rotation of the Earth slightly. Indeed, the Earth's spin is generally slowing because the moon's gravity is acting as a drag, so days are getting longer by about 1.7 milliseconds per century (although oddly, the Earth has recently started to spin faster again). Events such as El Niño and the moon's gravitational pull disturb the similarity between man-made time and more flexible time based on the Earth's naturally occurring rotation. When events like this happen, a bunch of humans you probably have never heard of (the International Earth Rotation and Reference Systems Service, should you wish to thank them) make the decision to add a small slice of time to your day, without your knowledge. We try to force our fixed, man-made view of time on to nature in the false hope that it will yield. It doesn't.

Nonetheless, we continue to hold our totally artificial view of time, and many aspects of daily life are now shaped by it. Companies pay their employees what they think their time is worth. Interest charges on loans and credit cards are nothing more than a fee for the length of time for which the money is borrowed. Prior to this twisted conception of time, early Christians banned usury, or charging interest on a loan, because time belonged to God and could not be bought or sold. In Islamic law, this practice is called *riba* and remains forbidden (although Islamic banks provide several workarounds, such as *murabaha*, which is the prior agreement of the markup of a product). Not only had humans created an artificial view of time by trying to add uniformity where there was none, but we also began to give this man-made imposter an overbearing presence in our lives. Just like the acquaintances of Tom Ripley had discovered, allowing dangerous fraudsters into your life is terrible news for your psychological and physical health.

The last few decades have seen the biggest changes in how we interact with time. It may be incomprehensible to Generation Z, but it was not too long ago in the UK that people frequently dialled a phone number sponsored by a watch company to get an accurate reading of the time (you can still reach a telephone speaking clock in the UK, but it is no longer common to do so). Now, as I sit at my desk, authoring this book, I can see the time on my laptop, desktop screen, mobile phone, office telephone and sports watch. All the timepieces are completely synchronous, because they are based on incredibly precise atomic clocks that keep time by monitoring the consistent wobble of an atom. All devices produced by Apple, for example, base their timekeeping on an atomic clock situated at the US Naval Observatory in Washington DC. The integration of clocks into our everyday items makes time omnipresent, ruling over us in a covert dictatorship. Some people even use apps that tell us what time to eat and drink, rather than doing so when we are hungry or thirsty. Time's favourite device of tyranny, however, is the dreadful alarm clock.

Despite their admirable dedication to spending hours with loved ones at the dinner table, the French seem particularly keen to create time-centric lifestyles that ruin our mojos. Not only did the Paris Observatory introduce the first telephone speaking clock in 1933, but the first patent for an alarm clock was developed by a Frenchman, Antoine Rédier, in 1847. This novel device soon spread around the world and had significant consequences. It is common nowadays to bemoan technological advances because they are reducing the need for humans to be employed. Robotic and artificial intelligence innovation in the manufacturing industry, for example, has reduced the need for human input on factory floors across the world. But situations like this one are not a new occurrence. Prior to the alarm clock, thousands of 'knocker-uppers' were employed in the UK and other countries to go from door to door, waking factory employees at their desired time. They used various tools, such as sticks and pea shooters, to fulfil their duties. In some industrial towns, miners would write the times of their shifts in chalk outside their homes so that the knocker-upper knew when to start tapping. The increasing availability of the alarm clock led to the extinction of the knocker-upper. What's more, the sound of the alarm clock has gone on to strike fear into millions of people across the world.

Jet lag, but not as we know it

Whether it be a pea striking your window or an alarm clock, aligning ourselves with man-made schedules rather than our natural biological rhythms is a harmful habit to develop. Anyone who has taken a long flight will have experienced jet lag. It occurs when your normal sleep pattern is disturbed after travelling across several time zones. After a few restless nights and some daytime fatigue, the effects usually disappear. However, in 2006, a potentially more serious type of jet lag was defined – *social jet lag*.[13] This phenomenon arises from a significant difference between our natural waking time based on our internal body clock and the time we actually wake up thanks to obligations like education or work. It is formally measured by calculating the average difference between the midpoint of our sleep before working days (or 'school nights') and days when we don't have commitments. For example, if you normally sleep from 11pm to 6am on a school night, and midnight to 9am on a work-free night, then your social jet lag is two hours (the difference between 2.30am and 4.30am). An easier way to establish whether you are suffering from social jet lag is to determine your reliance on an alarm clock on workdays. If you set an alarm as a precaution but usually wake up before it goes off or do not need one at all, then it is unlikely you are suffering from social jet lag. Many of us, however, wake abruptly when a hideous artificial noise says so, not when our biological clock tells us we have had enough sleep. Social jet lag is incredibly prevalent in industrialised countries. Seventy per cent of students and workers experience at least one hour per night of social jet lag, and almost fifty per cent experience two hours or more.[14]

A variation of social jet lag can also occur when your normal waking time is significantly earlier than sunrise, which presents a little-known problem in some countries. The further people live from the location that their region or country's time is based on, the more likely they are to have this type of social jet lag. This is not much of a problem in the UK, where nobody lives that far from Greenwich. Bristol, for example, is located two degrees west of Greenwich, which means 7am should really be 6.50am (this was the case before the standardisation of clocks). Ten minutes of social jet lag per night will not have significant consequences for Bristolians. But spare a thought for people residing in Chengdu in the Western Sichuan province of China. Since 1949, time in China has been entirely based on the sun's location in Beijing, which lies in the far east of the country. According to the sun, Chengdu time should deviate by several hours from Beijing time, but Chengdu inhabitants are constrained to living according to the sun in Beijing. When it's 7am in Beijing, it should be the middle of the night in Chengdu, yet it's also 7am.

The Chinese would really benefit from resorting back to having five different time zones. Trying to artificially modify time and ignore the sun's suggestion is bad for the health of their nation. The further west people live in any given time zone, the greater their risk of developing many diseases, including obesity, diabetes, heart disease and breast cancer.[15] This effect has been attributed to people in the west getting less morning light, which disrupts their natural body clock and leads to social jet lag. China's huge single time zone raises the prospect of some inhabitants living several hundred miles to the west of Beijing and get very little morning sunlight. Although China are the worst offenders, they are not the only country that falls into this trap. India also has a single time zone when they should have two.

Many societies also mess with time by moving the clocks forward, usually by one hour, during warmer months. There's good reason for what is commonly called 'daylight saving time'; it means evening darkness occurs later and jobs, such as farming, can continue a little longer. It also means social jet lag occurs across many parts of the world, because people wake up earlier than nature and their bodily rhythms would recommend. In 2011, Russia stopped changing their clocks back and forth to remain in daylight saving time, but then decided to shift the clocks back an hour to permanent standard time in 2014. Scientists happened to be monitoring young Russians' sleep patterns and mood during these transitions, which presented an opportunity to test what happens when we meddle with time.[16] The three years in permanent daylight saving time led to increased social jet lag and lower mood in the winter months. Messing with time in this way also disrupts the body's ability to regulate energy consumption. In other words, we struggle to consume the right types and amount of food when socially jet-lagged. This likely explains why social jet lag is associated with increased body mass index, waist size, and diseases related to weight, such as type 2 diabetes.[17]

Positive effects occur when we loosen our attachment to artificial time and let nature lead us. Many of us were forced to work from home during the Covid-19 pandemic. Although this arrangement was stressful for some, it meant avoiding the commute to work and adopting a more flexible start to the working day. Surveys from around the world demonstrated that people generally slept longer on workdays, more in line with how long they slept on work-free days. A seventy per cent drop in alarm-clock use was witnessed, and social jet lag was reduced by around an hour.[18] History and science have repeatedly shown that when we align our lives with nature's timing, whether that be the setting of the sun or our own biological clocks, we tend to be physically and psychologically healthier.

It is generally inconvenient to move across the country to align your sleep patterns with the sun, but social jet lag can be mitigated in other ways. The condition most likely occurs because sleep on school nights is not of sufficient quality or length, so individuals need to catch up on other days, usually the weekend. All the common sleep habit recommendations will help with this problem, including limiting screen time, alcohol or caffeine before bed on school nights. Getting some sunlight and exercise soon after waking up will also help your biological clock to develop a healthy rhythm. Sunlight helps

regulate serotonin and melatonin, both of which are important neurotransmitters that control our body clock.[19] Exercise
can also achieve this, albeit to a lesser degree.[20] Further
lifestyle modifications might be necessary on work-free days
when most people have more control over their time. You
could tone down the late-night partying or put the Saturday-
night film on sooner so that you naturally wake a little earlier
on work-free days. This isn't the sexiest piece of advice, but
it will be good for your health. It should also be used as a
general guideline rather than a strict rule (an occasional party
is good for most people's mojo). If you're in control of your
workday wake time, then replicate the pandemic and stay
in bed a little longer if it helps to align your sleep patterns.
Spending an extra few minutes snoozing is not lazy if it leads
to better health.

The fabricated attitudes to time developed by industrialised
nations and cultures have backfired, and there is little doubt
that time impacts our lives on a grand scale. Living according
to our alarm clocks, experiencing chronic levels of boredom,
and feeling constantly under time pressure have drastic consequences. People often talk about *having* time to do an activity.
Sometimes we *have* time to exercise, sometimes we do not.
Sometimes we *have* time to visit a friend, sometimes we do
not. 'I don't have time' is not only a poor excuse for inaction,
but also completely misleading. This phrase implies that we
have control of what we do with our time. I regret to tell
you that many of us need to wake up, rub the sleep from our
weary eyes and smell the single-origin Guatemalan coffee. We
do not have time, *time has us*, even if we largely do not notice
it. Time dictates what we do and when we do it. Most of us
do not wake up when we want to, but when time tells us to.

Most of us do not go to work when we feel like it, but when it's time to do so. We (usually) don't order a glass of Merlot at 10am, because it's the wrong time. We have little choice over when we die, we just exit the stage when our time is up. We cannot stop time, but time can – and often does – stop us. Make no mistake: time is our master. We must fight this oppression, defeat our tyrannical ruler, and become masters of time to restore our mojos.

Too many of us are allowing various features of time to destroy our health, squash our spirits and wreck our well-being. Time can also trample on our dreams and ambitions, preventing us from achieving anything of personal value and thwarting our healthy habits and behaviours. When we allow time to make these transgressions, our actions conflict with our core values. We get angry with those we love, feel apathy when we used to be enthused, and remove the joy from our lives. It is these related attacks by time on our mojos that this book aims to prevent. Mojo is characterised by *feeling* good and energised, while at the same time maintaining routines and *behaviours* that we personally value, which keep us healthy and help us develop. It's not easy progressing, developing, learning and achieving, while also being happy, relaxed and uplifted. I once had a chat with a gentleman at an airport who had an extremely successful career but understood he had neglected his family for years. He felt helpless to do anything about this situation. I've seen many parents with a beautiful family life, but their itch to regain their individual identity continually irritates and they feel like time is simply passing them by. Almost weekly, a sports news story will describe a supreme champion who has been mentally crushed by their efforts to get to the top because they have spent too little time supporting their wellbeing. Understanding time and developing a healthy relationship with it will harmonise the major aspects of your life, from personal development and professional achievements, to happiness, health and relationships, or any other context that is important to you.

Relationship therapy

Our relationship with time may be dysfunctional, but there are things we can do to break free and stop feeling like we live under time's tyranny. Chapter two of this book explains that having no time to nourish your soul and replenish your mojo in your life has nothing to do with how packed your schedule is. The feeling of frantic busyness is caused by disruptions in our *perception* of time. The brain is designed to manipulate our perception of time to benefit us, but it's often too concerned with trying to cope with stress, anxiety and life's curve balls to do so effectively. Subsequent chapters illustrate how time compels us to intend one thing but do the opposite. Time makes us feel like saints one moment and sinners the next. Time encourages us to chase our dreams but chains us to the sofa. Chapter three advises that you will probably fail to sustain any new, meaningful and spirit-enhancing activities if you expect willpower to perform over time. Chapter four explains that we frequently renege on our worthwhile intentions because we are wildly inaccurate at predicting the future. Chapter five illustrates how quitting and failure are common if time penetrates the gap between your actions and the outcomes that you desire.

Later chapters illuminate how important factors in shaping

your spirit and helping you achieve your goals change over time. Chapter six focuses on your recall of previous experiences. In contrast to what we might think, we do not assess entire experiences and events evenly, but recall different moments depending on their place in time. Chapter seven focuses on how our effort waxes and wanes predictably over time, and identifies key phases in a project or activity when different strategies are needed to initiate or maintain effort.

Time can also be a loyal sidekick if we allow it. Chapter eight emphasises the importance of time in solitude to enable creativity and original thinking, and to allow new features of your character to be awakened and flourish. Chapter nine encourages you to let time employ its healing powers when your mojo has gone on vacation. Chapter ten describes how spending some well-earned time to define and live your life according to your true identity is the essential characteristic of a regained mojo. Your core identity is a potent motivational weapon that can be employed to override the trickery of time, provide a large tonic for your mojo and allow you to sustain any hobbies, projects and lifestyle changes that you wish.

I have spent twenty years researching how motivation and wellbeing can simultaneously occur. As a result, I describe the scientific theory and evidence underpinning the ideas contained in this book, but I also dip into other fields, such as religion, literature, film, sport and business to elaborate on these ideas. Throughout this book, straightforward strategies are provided that will help improve your mojo. These strategies can be adapted to whatever aspect of your life requires attention, from business and personal finance to exercise, family life and new hobbies. This book is, therefore, relevant to anyone looking to get a little more out of their life, whether that be a CEO of a company or a full-time parent, an elite athlete or someone about to put on trainers for the first time. Some of the strategies will create a noticeable shift in your life from the moment you implement them. Others will make smaller contributions that you may not notice at first. All of them will cultivate your relationship with time, and help you understand how your brain works and how to get the most out of life.

2

Time warps

'Time is an illusion. Lunchtime doubly so.'

– Ford Prefect, fictional galactic hitchhiker

The phrase 'space-time continuum' conjures up images of intrepid time travellers hurtling through hyperspace and strange planets in galaxies far beyond our own reality. But the continuum is not a fantasy restricted to the imaginations of science-fiction enthusiasts. It is a fundamental principle in mathematics and physics. It forms the basis of much of what we understand about life. The work of two of the world's best-known scientists, Albert Einstein and Stephen Hawking, was heavily underpinned by the continuum, or 'spacetime', as physicists like to call it. Rather than a form of intergalactic voyage, spacetime is any mathematical model that combines time and the three dimensions of physical space into a single integrated concept.

Being based on the laws of physics and the formulae of mathematics, it would be sensible to assume that space and time are permanent and inflexible structures. In fact, this conclusion would be completely wrong. Imagine you are watching a friend who is standing on an airport travellator travelling from left to right. She then drops a golf ball. Your friend watches the ball drop *vertically* to the travellator floor, because she is moving at the same speed as the travellator. But from your viewpoint, the ball has travelled on a *diagonal* path downwards and slightly to the right, because your friend was moving that way. This is strange because the ball took an identical length of time to hit the floor, but travelled a longer distance from your viewpoint than your friend's. This means that the same ball travelled faster for you than for your friend. For many people experiencing a lack of mojo, the same could be said about life. A misplaced mojo is often characterised by a frantic feeling of busyness, where your own life feels like it is racing by seemingly much faster than everyone else's. This is accompanied by a feeling of being helpless to do anything about it.

Things get more bizarre if we were to switch the golf-ball scenario and keep distance and speed, rather than time, constant (remembering that time equals distance divided by speed). The ball would take less time to travel the same distance for you than for your friend. Indeed, the faster the travellator moves, the bigger the difference in perception of time between you and your friend. This effect is an example of *time dilation*, which was one of the foundational ideas behind Einstein's work. Time dilation also means that time passes more slowly for your head than your feet (when standing). The further away from the Earth's centre, the faster the speed as the Earth spins, which means time passes more slowly. The difference is incredibly small: a year would be about fifteen microseconds longer on the top of Mount Everest than if you were at sea level.

This effect will be familiar if you've seen the film *Interstellar*. The astronauts in the film don't age as much as characters who remain on Earth, because their speedy space travel means time passes slower than it does on Earth. If you were to hop in your spaceship and travel at ninety per cent of the speed of light for a year, your friends on Earth would have aged approximately two years and four months. Importantly for us, these examples of travellators, spinning worlds and space travel demonstrate that time is not stable but outrageously flexible. Our perception of time is altered depending on what we are doing and the perspectives we take. To restore our mojos and alleviate the busyness we often experience, we need to open our minds and embrace this fact. Not having enough time is one of the defining aspects of a lack of mojo. Are we so busy we don't have time for friends and family? Do we really have no time to exercise, read a book, dust off that musical instrument, sign up for a language course or learn a new skill? Are we too busy – or is it that our outlook and environment are making us *feel* too busy?

Take your nose off the grindstone

In many countries, a hard-working, dynamic life is viewed as a sign of success, but few of us have stopped to contemplate where this doctrine stems from, and whether it is of any use to us now. Whether you personally subscribe to a religion or not, religious texts continue to hold enormous influence over your life and the society that you live in. For example, we can observe the championing of hard graft in the Old Testament. God created Adam to get busy cultivating the Garden of

Eden. The Big Man played a blinder when he granted humans the Sabbath to rest and divert attention from the Monday-to-Saturday toil. Centuries later, the sixteenth-century monk Martin Luther advocated that work should be an obligatory duty, and the term 'Protestant work ethic' was born. A few hundred years later, philosopher and mathematician Thomas Carlyle emphasised that meaningful labour was essential for a healthy person and a healthy society. No wonder keeping your nose to the grindstone is viewed as admirable. And it is not just in our paid work that we should slog, either. A persistent reluctance for labour in all aspects of life – or sloth, as it is better known – is a cardinal sin. 'The devil makes work for idle hands', after all. We are programmed to view sustained endeavour as admirable, so we crack on and get busy.

This idea of busyness equating to success is an odd status signal that only became prominent in the last couple of centuries. In the UK period drama *Downton Abbey*, the matriarchal Dowager Countess of Grantham, Violet Crawley, asked 'What is a "weekend"?', revealing her ignorance of the difference between the leisurely Saturday-to-Sunday and the remainder of the week. This humorous quip was consistent with the real status signalling of that era. Then, unlike today, financial and societal prowess was demonstrated by *not* working. For example, a pale, smooth complexion was desired to signify that people didn't engage in hard outside labour. Prior to this era, in the late Middle Ages, exceedingly long and pointy shoes that were not suitable for work were worn by wealthy men for the same reason. Why on earth would you work if you were wealthy?

Fast-forward to the twenty-first century, and many industrialised cultures encourage us to promote how busy we are.

Social media is riddled with posts encouraging us to work as hard as Beyoncé in the studio or David Goggins in the gym. Friends relentlessly busy-brag when you ask them how they are. If you are not busy, then your life must be worthless or irrelevant. In the 1980s, 'moonlighting' referred to having a second job in addition to regular employment. It was typically frowned upon, because it seemed unethical or detrimental to the main job. Nowadays, having a second income is known as a 'side hustle' and is essential if you want to be seen as successful in some social circles. Advances in technology and an increase in working from home have also led many to feel unable to free themselves from the pressure to be productive, and they no longer know whether they are working from home or living at work. These pressures have led people to sell their time to employers as though it is cheap and limitless.

Busyness as a status symbol has been studied extensively by scientists. In one experiment, half the participants read about Jeff, a thirty-five-year-old man who works long hours and has a calendar that is always full.[21] The other half read about another Jeff, also thirty-five years old, but this Jeff does not work and has a leisurely lifestyle. In contrast to the post-Edwardian values conveyed in *Downton Abbey*, the first Jeff was deemed to have a much higher social status than the second. This belief was especially strong in participants who believed that success was based on hard work. In a second experiment, participants read about thirty-five-year-old Anne, who wore either a hands-free Bluetooth headset (to signify busyness) or listened to music through headphones (to signify leisure). The first Anne was rated as having a higher social status than the second, even after the researchers accounted for how expensive and innovative the headwear looked.

Researchers have also investigated whether busyness matches wealth as a status symbol. Some participants read about an individual who used an online shopping and delivery service, implying that they were busy. Others read about the same individual, except they bought expensive shopping brands, implying that they were wealthy. A third group of participants read that the individual shopped at an average grocery store as a comparison to the other two shoppers. The online shopper was perceived to be of a higher status than the average grocery store shopper, even though the two shopping methods were perceived to cost the same. Furthermore, the online shopper was deemed to be of the same social status as the luxury brand shopper. If you want to demonstrate status, being busy is as good as being rich.

Not all countries or cultures value busyness as an indicator of status. In a replication of the experiment involving the thirty-five-year-old Jeff, Americans were found to value busyness, but Italians valued leisure. Americans typically believe that hard work can lead to climbing the social hierarchy, but Italians do not hold this belief to the same extent. US citizens are a prime example of a monochronic society; they tend to live their lives by the clock, equating busyness with success and the American Dream. For Americans, time is money. Monochronic cultures view time as a quantifiable commodity, much like the Greenwich Observatory did in the nineteenth century. These cultures measure time in precise units to enable planning and management. Time can be spent or saved, but shouldn't be wasted. If you live in a country underpinned by a monochronic culture, like the US or UK, you probably haven't considered that an alternative perspective exists. We rarely sit down with a coffee and contemplate our temporal values, unless you are authoring a book about time.

But a different view of time does exist. Many Latin American, African, Asian and Arab cultures are underpinned by polychronic attitudes to time and busyness. Polychronic cultures believe that time is flexible. Schedules are guidelines rather than rules, and multitasking is favoured. A work meeting scheduled to finish at 11.15am while another one is due to start at 11am would not be out of the question. Time does not need to be monitored and traded so precisely, partly because it is impossible to know how long some activities will take. The length of time needed to build a business relationship between clients, for example, cannot be quantified. An appointment delayed by hours would largely go unnoticed. Many traditional cultures where an agricultural or hunter-gather lifestyle is still common also have conflicting approaches to busyness compared to monochronic countries. The Kapauku people living in Papua New Guinea do not typically work on two consecutive days, while traditions in other South Pacific Islands dictate that men only work four hours per day. Some communities living in the Kalahari Desert only work six hours per day, on two or three days per week.

The course of history also provides examples of nonconformists who didn't subscribe to the perspective that more toil means more success. Major industrial figures Henry Ford and W. K. Kellogg went against the grain and discovered that their employees were more productive when they worked less. Oscar Wilde advocated that: 'Work is simply the refuge of people who have nothing whatever to do.' Nobel Laureate Bertrand Russell authored a magnificent essay called 'In Praise of Idleness', in which he demolished many of the prevailing ideas about work and suggested that '. . . immense harm is caused by the belief that work is virtuous'. Several contemporary authors agree with these sentiments. In his 2017 book *Utopia for Realists*, Rutger Bregman dedicates a whole chapter to the benefits of the fifteen-hour working week. And you can guess what Tim Ferris's bestseller, *The Four-Hour Workweek*, concerns.

Some individuals have also been incredibly effective at protecting their time against people who want to take it. Allegedly, an English ambassador asked the leader of pre-war Germany, Otto von Bismarck, how he dismissed visiting statesmen who took up too much of his time. 'I have an infallible method,' said Bismarck. 'My servant arrives and informs me that my wife has something urgent to tell me.' Immediately after he said this, a servant entered with an urgent message from Bismarck's wife.

There are hopeful signs that change is on the way in work settings. In the US and Ireland, a four-day work week was implemented in various companies for six months in 2022 with very promising results. Employee stress, burnout, fatigue and work–family conflict all decreased over the course of the trial.[22] On the other hand, physical and mental health, work–life balance, and satisfaction in several areas of employees' lives increased. Ninety-seven per cent of all the employees wanted to continue with a four-day work week, and almost all the participating companies rated the trial a massive success. After a similar trial ended in over sixty UK firms in 2023, fifty-six continued with the four-day work week, and eighteen organisations made it a permanent policy.[23] What is most surprising, however, is that implementation of a four-day work week almost always maintains or increases productivity. Irish and US company managers were asked to rate how the four-day work week had impacted productivity, and the average score was nearly eight out of ten (0 = very negatively and 10 = very positively). These benefits to productivity were not achieved by employees speeding up and having to work until exhaustion during the other four days; they just worked smarter. A four-day work week makes people value their time appropriately. People plan better, identify priorities and don't feel the need to accept every meeting invitation. Counterintuitively, having less time made people put strategies in place that made them feel like they had more time.

We are joining those revolutionaries who view time and busyness differently in order to change how we interact with time in all aspects of our lives. We cannot add a little time to our days like the folk from chapter one who monitor the rotation of the Earth, but we can radically alter our perception of time. To be more precise, we can mend the warp in our perception of time that has left our mojos and motivation in tatters.

The illusion of busyness

For the majority, 'not having the time' is one of the most common barriers to making life changes. 'I haven't got time to cook properly', 'I haven't got time to exercise', 'I haven't got time to start a new business', 'If only I had the time to take up a new hobby'. When people declare that they do not have the time for something like exercise, they are being imprecise. If someone put a gun to their head and instructed them to complete ten star jumps or eat lead, they would miraculously find time to exercise. This example may seem pedantic and extreme, but it is essential to define the problem precisely. People have the time, but they *think* they do not, because they have other, higher priorities. When people feel this way, they often think they need to be more efficient and reach for various strategies aimed at becoming more productive. These tactics are generally designed with the goal of fitting more into one's life, but often create more time pressure, not less. In fact, many former proponents of uber-productivity and supremely efficient lifestyles, such as Tim Ferris in the US or Oliver Burkeman in the UK, are now turning their backs on these ideas and embracing a more balanced, mojo-filled life-style. The solution to not having enough time is to remove the feeling of time pressure, not to cram more activities in.

Scientists asked around 250 middle-aged women to keep a diary for seven days to track their daily activities.[24] As you'd expect, these diaries revealed that some women were extremely busy, spending most of their days working, looking after family and so on, while other women reported being much less busy. But this was not the interesting point about the investigation. The women were also asked whether they felt they had the time for physical activity in their schedules. Their responses revealed that actual time available had no relationship whatsoever to the perceived time available. In other words, *being* too busy and *feeling* too busy are very different, completely unrelated issues. *Being* busy is not the problem, and it does not stop us from making lifestyle changes or taking up new activities. *Feeling* busy is the driving factor behind a lack of time for anything meaningful or enjoyable.

Feeling overly busy can have dire consequences. Everyone knows that speeding in your car is dangerous. Speeding kills several hundred people on UK roads every year. Despite this ominous fact, two-thirds of UK drivers who responded to a survey said they break the speed limit if they are in a rush.[25] Put another way, six out of ten drivers would increase the probability of killing someone because they feel busy. Maybe the current state of *rush* hour – potentially the biggest misnomer ever created – is not such a bad thing. In central London, rush hour lasts for two hours, and the average speed for motor vehicles is approximately nine miles per hour.[26] This crawl means that a six-mile trip takes over forty minutes across central London. A good amateur runner would be able to run it in the same time. At least no one is likely to die at these speeds.

The distinction between being and feeling busy is why the phrase work–life balance is misleading. This expression falsely implies that you need equal measures of work and leisure in your life to feel energised. More important for your spirit is work–life *harmony*, which acknowledges that equal measures might be unnecessary and different people have different priorities at different points in their lives. In my younger years, I felt I had so much time that I could work sixty hours per week, have lots of opportunities for socialising, keeping fit and other activities, and still feel great. I was busy, but I didn't *feel* busy. If I attempted to work that many hours in a week now, it would make me *feel* very busy and out of control. Problems also occur when the people thriving on a sixty-hour week expect others to do the same without considering their individual circumstances. These types of work–life disharmony are catastrophic for wellbeing.

A survey undertaken in the US found a magical few – just less than ten per cent of survey responders – who reported having very little free time but also felt completely unrushed.[27] These people were *twice* as happy as everyone else who responded to the survey. They did not feel like they were on the relentless hamster wheel, but they had created a lifestyle that kept them active and thriving. These contented folk weren't from a particular demographic; there was a mix of married and single people, young and old, wealthy and poor. This assortment of individuals implies that anyone can hit the sweet spot and achieve a serene state of being busy without *feeling* busy.

One solution to feeling less frantic might be to copy the early Roman republic, who timetabled eight days per week. One of these days was ring-fenced for shopping. Life would be much easier if there was a day designated for going food shopping, ordering that essential item from Amazon and perusing the latest season's fashion. It was only when Rome embraced Christianity in the fourth century that the seven-day week was implemented. However, if there is no relationship between being and feeling busy, simply adding time to our calendars is unlikely to lessen the frantic feeling of busyness, so this strategy is not the answer. In any workplace, you'll find a colleague lamenting that they are completely overworked, yet they have managed to make their coffee break extend to ninety minutes. Giving these individuals more time or fewer tasks will not make them feel less busy.

A more realistic strategy is to manipulate our perceptions of time. A watched pot never boils, time drags like RuPaul when you are bored, and time flies when we are having fun. These phrases aren't just clichés; time seems to be abundant when we are waiting for something to happen, but disappears when we are not. Rather than time dictating when it enters or leaves

our lives, we need to be in the driver's seat. German physi-
ologist Karl von Vierordt is most famous for inventing the
sphygmograph, the first instrument that could measure blood
pressure without using invasive methods. Less well known
is the fact that he also noticed differences between people's
perceived length of time spent on a task and the actual time
taken. In what later became known as Vierordt's law, he suggested that short intervals are more likely to be overestimated
(e.g., five seconds feels like six seconds), while long intervals of
time tend to be underestimated (e.g., five years feels like four
years). But this perspective is overly simplistic. Sometimes an
hour feels like ten minutes, and sometimes it feels like two
hours. Our perception of time is totally flexible, and its direction and flow seemingly haphazard.

How do we warp time?

To understand why our perception of time passing varies so
much, we can turn to William James, widely recognised as
the godfather of American psychology. He gained an eclectic
education studying art, physiology, medicine, psychology and
philosophy. It was while studying at Harvard University that
James became a member of an informal gentlemen's group
called The Metaphysical Club. The collective contained a
renowned novelist, a future Supreme Court Justice, and
several philosophers who went on to shape American society and influence presidents. These guys knew their onions,
so we should take their advice. James's nineteenth-century
masterpiece, *The Principles of Psychology*, contains more
than twelve hundred pages of physiology, psychology and

philosophy. Within it, he succinctly wrote: 'our feeling of time harmonises with different mental moods'. The key to becoming the master of time and bending it back into shape is our underlying emotional state. As we counterintuitively discovered in the four-day work-week trials, giving employees less time at work made them *feel* better and like they had more time to get things completed. Emotions will control your outlook on time if you let them – or they can be harnessed to improve your life.

There is no single part of the brain that is responsible for how we experience time, but it helps to think about an internal clock. Our emotional state alters the speed of our internal clock compared to real time, making our perception of time vary accordingly. Until recently, scientific efforts to understand the relationship between emotions and time perception had been contradictory and confusing. The picture cleared somewhat when scientists began to examine the motivational properties of our emotions.[28] Emotions that motivate us *towards* a goal or outcome are called 'approach-orientated emotions'. These emotions can have positive undertones, such as when we desire something or enjoy progressing towards a goal. They can also have negative undertones, like when we get angry and try to change something. In an approach-orientated emotional state, much of the brain's attentional resources are dedicated to an activity, and very little resource gets allocated to our internal clock. This causes the internal clock to slow down, and makes real time seem to pass quickly. For example, imagine that you are totally absorbed in reading a fabulous book (hopefully, this is not difficult to imagine currently), or that you're determined to get a frustrating work project completed. An hour passes, but your internal

clock has moved on by only ten minutes, so time seems like
it has flown by (an hour seemed like ten minutes). The same
thing occurs when you have a desire for something. If I were
to show you something enticing, like a tasty-looking dessert,
and something neutral, like a cube (assuming you do not find
cubes desirable), for the same length of time, you would probably think that the dessert had been displayed for a shorter
amount of time, especially if you were hungry.[29] Your brain's
resources would be employed to focus on the object of desire
and away from your clock, so what would feel like a few seconds would really be a little longer. This process would not
occur when looking at a cube.

The reverse happens in circumstances when our emotions
deter us from something, usually a threat. These emotions are
called 'avoidance-orientated emotions'. When we experience
these emotions, basic survival systems are triggered, and it's
helpful for your internal clock to speed up so that real time
seems like it has slowed. Imagine you hear two sounds for
the same length of time, one a bloodcurdling shriek and
the other a flirty giggle. You are more likely to perceive the
shriek as lasting longer because it's likely to trigger avoidance-
based emotions, like fear. You are also likely to overestimate
the time spent observing horrible and extreme images, like
crushed heads and eye tumours that make you feel disgusted.[30] This distortion of our experience of time means
we can react as fast as possible and avert danger. Imagine a
bullet moving towards you like in the *Matrix* films, or a final
devastating punch being thrown in slow motion like in the
Rocky films. These Hollywood analogies are an exaggeration
to illustrate the real-world effect of avoidance-based emotions
decelerating time.

Crucially, the way you interpret an event influences whether you experience approach- or avoidance-based emotions and, therefore, your perception of time. This means that the same experience can speed up time for one person and slow it down for another. If you approach a skydive with dread, a typical avoidance-orientated emotion, it will feel like it lasts longer than if you approach it with approach-orientated excitement.[31]

An example of time warping has been seen on reality TV. For over twenty years in the UK and many other countries, there has been a television show called *I'm a Celebrity ... Get Me Out of Here!*. If you are not familiar with the concept, celebrities of varying degrees of fame live together in a rudimentary jungle environment for several weeks, competing to be crowned King or Queen of the Jungle. The celebrities take on challenges to obtain food and treats for the group, while also attempting to avoid being voted out by viewers during their stay. In the 2023 'All Stars' edition, one of these challenges involved contestants placing their hands and feet in secure boxes, and an oversized fishbowl container being placed on their head.

The final three contestants were Jordan Banjo, a professional dancer with the group Diversity; Myleene Klass, a former pop star and now radio and TV presenter; and Fatima Whitbread, the 1987 world champion in javelin. The first part of the challenge involved thousands of critters, such as snakes, bugs, worms and beetles, being emptied into the containers so that the celebrities' hands, feet and heads were covered. The goal of the challenge was for the celebrities to estimate when six minutes had passed and hit a button. Only when all three contestants had pressed their button would the contestants be released from their torture. Having snakes wrapped round your head and insects crawl into most orifices is likely to trigger avoidance-orientated emotions in some people. Importantly, however, the three finalists had demonstrated that they could focus on achieving a goal, despite such circumstances, so they were very likely experiencing approach-orientated emotions. For example, all three had previously shown their prowess in putting their hands inside holes crammed with creepy-crawlies. In this situation, few resources would have been dedicated to their internal clock. This means that six minutes would pass, but their internal clock would move on much slower, and it would feel like less time has passed.

This is exactly what occurred. Jordan Banjo was first to press the button, at six minutes and thirty-four seconds. Next was Myleene Klass, but she didn't press the button until eleven minutes and twenty-eight seconds had passed. Staggeringly, Fatima didn't hit her button until fifteen minutes and ten seconds had elapsed. For Fatima, every two and a half minutes that went by felt like one minute. Hypothetically, if different celebrities attempted the challenge who were not able to focus on the objective and just wanted to get out, then their avoidance-based emotions would have slowed time and they would have pressed the button too early (although the likelihood would be that their emotions would have led them to quit irrespective of perceived time).

These time-warping processes function effectively when we are thriving. Time flies when we are engaged in activities, but identification of a rare threat that needs avoiding slows time so we can react accordingly. Crucially, a balanced, mojo-filled life also provides ample time when we are not driven by achieving goals *or* avoiding threat. We accomplish a few

things, then step out of the rat race and shift down a gear for
a little while. This neutral state allows time to progress neither
quickly nor slowly. Sadly, for many, work is stressful, home
life is frantic, and there's a constant pressure to be productive.
The treadmill never stops, and we live in a situation where
we are constantly 'on the go', trying to achieve things or solve
problems – just not the right things, or the right problems. We
are not absorbed in a fabulous new book or an exciting new
hobby like we could be. Instead, we are constantly immersed
in suboptimal goals, like combatting the sources of our anxiety, pressure, frustration and worry. With this mindset, we
are drowning in approach-orientated emotions, especially
ones with negative connotations, and we cannot switch off.
Excessive amounts of the brain's resources are needed to
constantly cope with and try to solve our issues, so we divert
resources away from our internal clock, and time seems to
fly. Before we know it, the morning has gone, and all we have
accomplished is writing 'Things to do today' at the top of
an empty page. It feels impossible to add another activity to
such a hectic day. Perceived lack of time is controlling many
people's lives, purely because they are unhappy and stressed.
Their baseline day-to-day emotional state is creating the
illusion of time flying by, and they feel manically busy, irrespective of how busy they actually are.

Our perception of time does slow occasionally, but not to
save us from a real threat to life, because they rarely exist anymore. Instead, time slows because we try to avoid completely
self-imposed, artificial threats. We experience avoidance-
orientated emotions because the work meeting becomes a
chance to be embarrassed in front of colleagues, the exercise
class becomes an opportunity to look fat, the school run is a

chance to compare badly to the other parents. Our systems that were designed to slow time when a real threat is identified and needs to be avoided are activated needlessly.

Imagine how squeezed your daily schedule would feel if time flew by and only slowed to focus on potential embarrassments or possible rejections. Your internal clock is swinging wildly between racing at breakneck speed and sporadically going unnecessarily slowly; it's never just at the right speed for the right moments. This would make most people feel extremely busy and out of control too. Welcome to the world of an individual who has lost their mojo. Being stressed, worried, unhappy and anxious creates the perfect cocktail to wreck your life. Malfunctioning emotional states distort your perception of time and fuel your feelings of busyness. No room or energy is left for activities that nourish the soul.

The underlying reasons for misplacing your mojo are unimportant. It could be a specific reason, like a work project or a family issue that has stressed you out and damaged your emotional state. Or it could emerge from something more chronic, like being stuck in an unfulfilled life or having low self-esteem. The essential thing to recognise is that you have become stuck in a cycle of destruction. You lose some sparkle, which warps your perception of time so that you begin to feel too busy and lacking in energy, which chips away at your wellbeing some more. Feeling chronically overwhelmed also damages how your body functions, especially the nervous system and endocrine system (the part that controls hormones). For example, when feeling overwhelmed or burnt out, hormones trigger a reduction of blood flow to the parts of the brain that help make rational decisions.[32] Neural connections are disrupted so that we fall back on habitual behaviours rather than behaviours that help us meet our goals.[33] In other words, feeling overwhelmed leads to poor decision-making, and keeps us stuck in our existing ways. Recalibrating these biological and psychological systems is essential if you are to feel less busy.

Rebuilding your emotional foundations

The recommendation to work on your emotional wellbeing is a little circular. To support your emotional wellbeing, you need to feel like you have some time. To feel like you have some time, you need to support your emotional wellbeing. This mutual relationship means there's no single solution to target; we just need to interrupt the circle at any point. Equally, there'll never be a perfect time to start fixing your mojo, so it's important to start now by making small changes. There are several well-trodden ways to work on your emotional wellbeing, like counselling, meditation, journaling and physical activity, to name a few. Try these strategies and add some of the more time-focused tactics described below. Think of these different tactics as tools in a box, with different ones suited to different challenges.

Protecting your time

A sudden, substantial change to your schedule is unlikely, unsustainable and unnecessary. When you're feeling overwhelmed, small changes are more likely to seem acceptable, and can be very effective. Begin by protecting your time as vigorously as Otto von Bismarck with those fake messages from his wife.

Almost all emails, messages and phone calls are people asking for your time. The simple act of considering the message takes time, never mind that you are also likely to be asked to commit to something that is unimportant to you. *Can you complete this form? Can you give me a call, it's important? What can you do about this issue? Can you contact HR?* Accessing your emails creates work. Only consider these requests when *you* are ready. Turn off the notifications for messages on your phone. Deactivate that little symbol on your computer that tells you an email has arrived – or, even better, sign out. Actively decide on periods when you are open to requests and read your messages then, not when your colleague thinks it's the right time to tell you about their work project.

Emails are the lowest form of work activity that exists. In fact, reading and responding to emails is often done to avoid real, meaningful work. Some people have been observed to check their emails thirty to forty times per hour.[34] Not only is it impossible to fully concentrate on meaningful work with this amount of distraction, but email dependence has also been associated with poor mental health and even reduced functioning in some areas of the brain.[35] Never ever try to be an 'admin ninja' and clear your emails or achieve 'inbox zero'. This latter phrase was coined by writer Merlin Mann, and referred to the desired amount of time a person's attention should be focused on their inbox. In its original guise, this phrase represented an admirable aim of not attending to emails at all. It has now been distorted into the ludicrous idea of trying to achieve no emails in your inbox. Attempting to reach inbox zero will probably take a significant amount of time for most people. We are trying to add time to our lives, not subtract it. Neglecting an email for a few days often makes the issue that it concerned go away, without any intervention from you. If you start responding to emails more slowly, you will often receive an email saying something like, 'Hi, can you help me out with ...' and then, a day later, 'Don't worry, problem sorted.' People often find different answers to their issues if you don't reply.

Staying on the subject of work, nobody should ever be scheduling meetings that finish on the hour, because that last five to ten minutes of every hour is *your* time to recalibrate. If a meeting suddenly appears in your online diary that finishes immediately before another one starts, then change the scheduling (and lambast the idiot who put it in there; privately, if it's your boss). These micro periods not only allow you to schedule a little time for you, but they also introduce some calmness to your life. A couple of minutes to get out of your chair and take a few deep breaths can make you feel temporarily less busy. Small changes like these won't give you the extra time to begin a new exercise regime or business venture, but that is not the aim at this point. The aim is taking back control of your time and addressing significant emotional imbalance. Identify all the methods, such as email, WhatsApp and work meetings, that people use to steal your time. Take control of them.

Recognising dead time

The next step is to heed the advice of ancient Roman philosopher Seneca.

> 'We're tight-fisted with property and money, yet think too little of wasting time, the one thing about which we should be the toughest misers.'

In one of his gloomier moments, he also advised:

'Whatever time has passed is owned by death.'

Combining these two pearls of wisdom implies that we are thoughtless when giving away our time. Identify periods of 'dead time', when you gain nothing from how you are spending your time, and start to use them more prudently. Wallowing in bed is one of the four most common forms of dead time. My alarm used to go off at 6.15am, but I frequently stayed in bed until much later, when it was time for my daughter to get up. This period wasn't useful; I just lay there thinking how tired I was or how to tackle some tasks while fixing neither. I was giving my time to Death for free. If you have time like this, then put it to better use. The major aim of removing small periods of dead time at this point is not to be more productive. Don't get sucked into the optimised living idea, where every moment of your life must be productive. Greater gains can be made by using this time to recalibrate your psychological and biological states with simpler things like making a cup of tea, taking some deep breaths and having a big stretch. The important thing is not to wallow in an ocean of dread.

As well as the beginning of your day, look out for dead time in the evening. A period of relaxing before bedtime is worthy, but this shouldn't be three hours spent slouched on the couch, floundering. If you are simply waiting for bedtime as soon as dinner is over, then that's dead time and needs to be removed. A key signal of evening dead time is channel-hopping or scrolling through a streaming channel's home page in the hope of finding something interesting to occupy your anxious mind. Don't think about starting major new things in the evening (see chapter three for the reason why); try something small and relaxing, like reading a book, listening to music or going for a walk, which should all provide a small, but significant tonic for your emotional state.

Mindlessly scrolling through social media without a purpose is the third and perhaps most common form of dead time. If you're going to do something so aimless, then at least combine it with something useful, like stretching a part of your body that hasn't properly functioned since your teenage years. Searching through social media can be a form of purposeful exploration at first, but can soon change into something less worthy. If you're going to dive in and explore TikTok, at least explore with a purpose. Find out the best way to chop an onion or discover a new holiday destination – but then stop. Having a reason or goal for your scrolling will prevent you from being sucked down a social media scroll-hole. Alternatively, you can ration your social media use or TV watching so you do not get hypnotised by the algorithm's suggestion that you might like to watch people mow lawns.

Finally, although the work commute by car, train or bus is technically not dead time because there is the explicit aim of getting to work or getting home, it's often a period where worry can consume you – and it's time that can be put to better use. Remove it from your life, if possible, by working from home or moving closer to your work so you can cycle or walk. These types of active commuting do not seem to provide the same opportunity for your worries to consume you. If it's not possible to remove suboptimal forms of commuting, then fill it with something that takes your mind away from anxiety. Learn a language, listen to a worthwhile podcast, or listen to the newest Taylor Swift album. At the risk of being repetitive, the important thing is not to wallow in an ocean of dread.

Viral emotions

A more drastic change to address your underlying wellbeing and change your perception of time is also worth considering. Thanks to the global events of the last few years, most people are well versed in how viruses spread. Less well known is that, just like viruses, emotions are also infectious. In the same way that some people catch and transmit colds more than others, people also differ in their ability to catch and transfer emotions. Some people have the emotional equivalent of a poor immune system and are easily infected by other people's emotions. Others might have the equivalent of poor sneezing etiquette and easily transmit their emotions to others.

Emotions can be transferred through voice. Happy people, for example, typically produce sounds with large variation in pitch and a fast tempo, but very little variation in amplitude.[36] When individuals hear these different vocalisations, there is not only a tendency to mimic them, but people also genuinely experience the emotional state contained in the message that was sent. This process occurs because copying the emotional signals of others sends feedback via the nerves to the brain that you are experiencing that emotion too.[37] Emotions can also be transferred through facial expressions, posture and movement. However, technology is changing the way emotions are transferred. We no longer have to physically meet people to catch their emotional state, because emotions are contagious across cyberspace. In a massive experiment involving nearly 700,000 Facebook users, researchers manipulated the type of emotional content in people's news feeds.[38] When people read less positive content from other people, their posts followed suit. The reverse pattern was observed when the experimenters reduced the negative posts.

Being able to 'catch' people's emotions has several advantages. The ability to observe others and pick up on their emotions and reciprocate is a key communication skill and will enhance social bonds. It is the basis for better empathy and being able to read a situation or room accurately and quickly. For new parents, accurately picking up on emotional states is a necessity, because babies have not yet mastered language. Despite these advantages, emotional transference is not beneficial if we are surrounded by overly busy people. Just like other psychological states, busyness and the associated feelings of being overwhelmed and stressed are infectious. The people and environments around you (including online) are a major reason why you feel too busy and overwhelmed. If your physical and online lives are full of people feeling too busy, you will feel too busy, too, especially if you are an empathetic person skilled in absorbing the emotions of others. If you are surrounded by people feeling overly busy on the Northern Line at 8am, then you are likely to feel that way too.

Who are the work colleagues, friends and family members who suck you in to a tornado of rush, haste and speed? Do you have a partner, family member or friend who expects immediate responses when they message or call you? If you do, that needs to change so you can take back control of your time. The optimal but extreme solution is to remove these people from your daily activities. Stop messaging your friend who is constantly dropping their busyness into your conversations. Change your lunchtime routine to avoid the colleague always floundering in busyness. A work colleague of mine once used the phrase 'A hole is better than an asshole' to describe the danger of recruiting an inappropriate person just to fill a job role. Your social life and work life would also improve if you heeded this wisdom. Don't fill your life with people who suck your spirit, just to gain so-called friends.

It may be difficult to take this option in some circumstances, especially if the individual transmitting their busyness to you is a loved one or a cherished friend. Situations like these require new expectations to be communicated. Inform the individual that you will be using your phone or email less and to expect slightly tardier responses from now on. If they respond negatively to this suggestion, you may have a bigger problem, because this sounds like neediness.

You can also adapt other virus avoidance tactics. At several periods during the Covid-19 pandemic, we were instructed to implement various strategies (e.g., meeting people outside) to reduce the likelihood of infection. In the same way, we manage the situations in which we meet friends to reduce the likelihood of emotional infection. Meeting people in a group often lessens the amount of emotional baggage one individual can transmit to you. In contrast, agreeing to a one-to-one over a flat white is the emotional equivalent of inviting someone to sneeze in your face.

Analysing your routine

Even if a small degree of emotional rebalance is achieved, you will be amazed at how much better – and less busy – you feel. These small changes will then allow you to start thinking with more clarity about the tasks and activities that you currently do in a day. An imaginative analysis of your routine is the second phase to changing your perspective of time and regaining your mojo. This change will further redress the imbalance in your emotional state, because you will feel like you have more time. Examining your routine can be approached in different ways.

Many of us are familiar with Parkinson's law, which states that work expands to fill the time allocated to it. Most of the time, this law is perceived as an annoyance to explain why things take longer than they should. However, we can apply the principle in reverse to create time too. If you have scheduled a meeting for one hour, try doing it for thirty minutes next time. You'll get the same amount done in this meeting, with much less waffle. If you usually plan to go to the gym for one hour, try going for forty-five minutes. You'll get the same workout, but will dither less between exercises. This principle can also be applied when you need to make a decision. If you need to choose new handles for your kitchen doors, it could take two hours to decide between brushed brass and chrome if you let it. Give yourself fifteen minutes, and you're very likely to come to the same decision as you would if you took longer.

To help formalise, prioritise and protect these small but significant chunks of time, consider diarising them. Most people use a diary, even if it's only for work purposes and not for personal life. Ideally, it should be a real paper diary to avoid your notifications and all those messages from people trying to take your time away from you. Counsellors often suggest using different colours for different life contexts to make it easier to identify whether one type of activity is dominating the others. Importantly, there need to be frequent chunks in your chosen colour signifying periods where you do not have any social commitments or obligations, and can focus on restoring emotional balance and mojo. Do not use this time as a buffer zone just in case other things overrun; treat it as sacred. Scheduling nothing is not the same as not scheduling anything. These periods need to exist as standalone activities, and should be viewed as one of your more important appointments.

Having a diary or a schedule also helps you routinise certain activities. The French novelist Gustave Flaubert suggested: 'Be regular and orderly in your life [...] so that you may be violent and original in your work.' Having a consistent routine will give your brain a rest and make you feel less busy because you do not need to weigh up competing priorities and decide whether to sacrifice one for the other. Taking your child to a swimming lesson every Thursday at 5pm is much easier than having to decide every week whether swimming, tennis or piano lessons are more important. Scheduling a work meeting with your team at the same time removes the mental load associated with switching activities around to fit it in.

Diarising can also help you identify overly frequent tasks. In most circumstances, repetitive tasks are not sufficiently important that you can't extend the cycle. Do you know what will happen in most circumstances if you have a fortnightly catch-up with your team instead of a weekly meeting?

Nothing. Do you really think that you will drown in a sea of dust if you don't polish your shelves on a weekly basis? Stretch the regularity of repetitive tasks.

Restorative activities

The aim of shrinking activities in this way is to provide some breathing space for restoration and to reduce the *feeling* of busyness. If you are lucky enough to feel that you now have some space to add an activity or two, then only things that enthuse you are permitted. It can be difficult to differentiate between activities that are truly restorative and obligations that make you feel equally as frantic or withered. Fortunately, over fifty years of research has identified that restorative activities need to contain some combination of three specific psychological ingredients.[39] First, an activity must make you feel capable or effective. If you start playing a new sport but it makes you remember being picked last during PE classes, then this will not restore your mojo. Second, it is helpful if an activity leads you to create or develop social bonds with others. This can happen overtly, like chatting to your best friend over coffee. Or it can happen covertly, like being part of a wider community that you are not necessarily in direct contact with.

The third ingredient is perhaps the most abstract. Restorative activities need to come from within your own mind. The activity cannot be done because you feel like it *should* be done, or because it feels like an obligation or coercion. You need to find your own activities, not activities that your friends or a book about time suggest you should do. You need to feel like you are the captain of your own ship. If the activity feels like something that you want to do, rather than something that you should do, then it comes from within and will be restorative. If your activities do not lead to affiliation, capability or a sense of ownership, then they will suck your mojo, not replenish it.

In a nutshell

Our perceived lack of time has nothing to do with how busy we really are. Our feelings of busyness and being out of control are simply a consequence of our underlying emotional state. Trying to continually solve problems and be productive creates emotions that make time whizz by. Our lives only slow when we have the chance to feel rejected, embarrassed or fearful. The link between our emotions and sense of time has developed over millennia but now malfunctions, so we must improve our emotional state to improve our sense of available time. As well as the traditional ways of improving your wellbeing, take control of your technology and guard yourself against all the methods that people use to take some of your time. Emails, phone messages and social media feeds should be accessed only when you are ready to give away some time. Identify the people in your social networks who are transmitting their busyness to you and guard against their emotional viruses.

Once we have recalibrated our emotions to some degree, we are more likely to have the mental space needed to examine our routines and make small changes. Remove or replace dead time, shrink the time needed for certain activities, develop routines and focus on adding restorative activities that nourish the soul. These activities will help you carve out a small slice of time, reduce feelings of busyness and begin to help you regain your mojo. This process is an important foundation step towards building a modified and sustainable lifestyle, not a temporary month-style or week-style.

3

Why do mousetraps work?

'I can resist everything, except temptation.'

– Oscar Wilde, illustrious playwright and bon viveur

Willpower. Restraint. Self-control. Only people blessed with these attributes can accomplish anything worth striving for, right? Countless temptations and diversions must mean that willpower is essential if we want to achieve our goals. Every dieter must battle an army of junk-food restaurants. Every money-saver must combat global brands with multi-million-pound advertising budgets. Every hopeful exerciser must struggle against the lure of the sofa. It is fortunate that our social media is bursting with emotive messages that inspire us to resist temptation, use willpower, and not to quit. Sadly, these noble efforts to keep you strong-willed are misguided. Common understanding of willpower and our ability to resist temptation is wrong. We must stop relying on willpower to lose weight, get fit, save money, write a book, or whatever positive steps in our lives we are trying to take. Relying on willpower allows time to do its dirty work.

The fragility of human resolve against temptation

represents one of the core themes in ancient religion, myth and legend. The story of Adam and Eve is among the most famous of biblical tales. Adam was created from the dusty earth and Eve fashioned from one of his ribs. The two fell in love and were told they could blissfully roam naked around the Garden of Eden for eternity, on the sole condition that they refrained from eating the forbidden fruit. Imagine being in their shoes (if they wore any), pondering this conundrum. You can live your best life forever, eat all the fruit that you desire, just not *that* fruit from that single tree over there. Easy, you might think. But with an irksome serpent whispering in Eve's ear, these pioneers of humanity could not resist temptation. Before you know it, they had succumbed to the urge to eat the forbidden fruit and shame engulfed them. The couple were banished from the Garden and sent to Earth, where they would toil and suffer like all humans do now. I wonder if they ever looked back and considered their life choices.

Like the story of the first man and woman, curious Pandora from Greek mythology could not resist opening the forbidden box – and, before she knew it, sickness, death and evil were released into the world (thanks a million, Pandora). In Islam, the angels Harut and Marut could not understand why God lauded weak-willed humans. In response, Allah challenged them to do better at resisting temptation. They defied all urges, until they met the beautiful Zohra. The two angels craved intimacy with her, but she refused unless they consumed alcohol. In the blink of an eye, the pair were downing liquor and revealing the sacred name of God. At least they had each other for the walk of shame back home. In more recent times, Hollywood adores the topic of human weakness against temptation, usually for sex, money and status. Despite these continuous examples over thousands of years, warnings about the pitfalls of relying on willpower in the hope of resisting temptation continue to fall on deaf ears.

Scientists generally agree that willpower, or self-control, is the ability to resist an immediate temptation in favour of a future valued goal. A common illustration of this definition is dieting to lose weight. Imagine you are trying to lose a few pounds to look fabulous at next month's grand social event. However, today is a work colleague's birthday, and they have provided doughnuts that are big enough to sit on and float down the River Nile. Some are even smothered in your favourite glaze (feel free to replace the doughnut in this scenario with your preferred indulgence). Eating a doughnut represents an immediate temptation that requires willpower to resist if you are to persist with your weight-loss goal. Another example is a boring but important work task, which requires willpower to complete it despite the temptation to scroll through Instagram instead. In both cases, willpower is required to *prevent* us doing something; however, willpower can also be employed to *do* something. Imagine you intend to exercise one evening, but you are currently reclining on your sofa, as comfy as a baby at its mother's bosom. Your favourite boxset is playing, and a velvety-smooth hot drink is in your hand. Willpower is likely required to fulfil your intention to exercise.

These three examples demonstrate that tests of willpower come in different guises. They could be intense, short-lived conflicts, like resisting a sweet treat or fighting to get off the sofa. They could also be a war of attrition, like completing a boring work task. Although these examples are different, when brain scans are taken during dilemmas like these, the brain activity shown is surprisingly similar. This research tells us that we can apply our general understanding of willpower to many different situations involving a temptation that conflicts with a personally valued goal.[40]

The above examples portray willpower as a worthwhile asset. Likewise, most people think of willpower as a virtue, and catchy slogans like Nike's 'Willpower knows no obstacles' and NiQuitin's 'Long live your willpower' have further spread the idea that willpower is necessary for success. When asked about their journeys to the top, Olympic champions and successful entrepreneurs often recall the times they dragged themselves out of bed despite the temptation to crawl deeper under the duvet. These events make a good anecdote, but their success was likely based on the many other days when getting up was consistently straightforward, not the occasional day when motivation was flagging. People may recall instances when willpower was successfully employed to resist temptation or overcome a barrier, but emphasising specific events is missing the point. It is possible to successfully employ willpower, but repeated or sustained reliance on its use will eventually grind your commitment into dust. Lasting progress and success do not stem from constantly requiring willpower. To explain why willpower is overrated and not the cornerstone of success it is thought to be, we need to look at human evolution.

The evolution of willpower

The rapid industrialisation in many countries over the last two centuries has seen unimaginable changes to our environment.

Prior to this period, keeping someone called Alexa in a tiny box and asking her questions would have led to accusations of lunacy, and probably imprisonment. In contrast, human biology has evolved at an incredibly slow pace. This discrepancy has caused many contemporary problems and illnesses. A proneness to storing fat used to be a biological advantage during frequent periods of food scarcity. Now, that same ability partly explains why significant numbers of us are living with obesity and at much greater risk of all sorts of nasty conditions. A tendency to crave and conserve salt was an advantage because dehydration was common in previous eras. Nowadays, excessive salt intake means nearly a third of Americans and Britons have high blood pressure.[41] It is the same story for the human brain. The pace of evolutionary development in the brain is so slow that the core functions of the brain work in an almost identical way to our distant lineage. It is these differences in biological and environmental development that explain why willpower should never be relied upon.

Our distant primate ancestors who lived millions of years ago were solitary creatures who didn't need much. Their requirements consisted of food and water, an occasional mate, and to avoid any predators or other threats to life. Important life goals, such as wanting to lose a few pounds or build a successful business did not enter the minds of our prehistoric predecessors. Although this lifestyle was straightforward, it was also difficult, so most decisions were dedicated to achieving these few basic aims. This existence continued for millions of years, which enabled the part of the human brain called the limbic system to evolve. This brain region excelled at motivating us to eat, have sex, run away from bigger animals – and little else. One of the ways it achieved this goal was to signal for the release of dopamine, a hormone which makes us feel good, when we see an opportunity to satisfy one of these needs. This reward encouraged us to repeat the process again and again. Willpower did not exist because there was never a need to resist temptation. If our ancestors had an opportunity to eat, then they ate.

These distant ancestors were mainly active at night because they could move quietly on their own to hunt prey and avoid predators. This lifestyle is thought to have persisted until a substantial change occurred approximately fifty-two million years ago.[42] Our ancestors began to be active during the day because they needed to travel faster and further to discover food more easily. However, this development meant they lost the advantage of being difficult to spot, so potential predators could attack them and prey could evade them more easily. The solution to this problem became one of the essential features of humanity. Our distant ancestors began to live in social groups to deter predators from attacking, and to hunt more successfully thanks to strength in numbers.

While this new adaptation to communal living was extremely successful, it presented a dilemma for our lineage. Two options were now available to enhance their chances of survival. They could still prioritise the immediate satisfaction of their established basic drives for survival, but relying on this tactic too much would harm their group membership and long-term chances of thriving. Alternatively, they could sacrifice their immediate basic urges in the hope that group membership would pay long-term dividends for their own survival. In other words, our ancestors' selfish brains were wired to take other people's food, mates and shelter if the chance arose, but now this would lead to being ostracised from these new social groups, meaning chances of survival would be reduced. But the primate brain was only designed to encourage the former strategy, not the deliberative decision-making required for the latter. In this new social structure, an individual may have wanted the food of a fellow group member, but if the companion in question was the best hunter, then allowing them to eat may have led to better chances of survival. And so, our ancestors evolved several abilities that helped them negotiate the complexities of living with others, including the ability to subdue urges and resist temptation for the benefit of goals that were not immediately valuable. This ability was the first, primitive version of willpower.

Exerting willpower and other related functions, such as cooperation and weighing up the pros and cons of different actions, became such valuable abilities that human ancestors developed an area of the brain called the prefrontal cortex (the bit directly behind your forehead), which was responsible for employing them.[43] Although parts of the prefrontal cortex can be found in other animals, no other species has one of the same relative size and complexity as ours.[44] Indeed, willpower and being able to inhibit natural urges are key psychological differences between humans and other primates. Parents of teenagers will also be unsurprised to discover that development of the prefrontal cortex is uniquely slow compared to other parts of the brain, with full maturity not occurring until early adulthood. Don't blame your teens when they consume the entire weekly food shop in two days.

The evolution of willpower allowed our ancestors to sacrifice immediate urges for long-term benefit, but total reliance on this method didn't always pay dividends. Sometimes our ancestors needed to submit to basic urges. A fellow group member may be the best hunter, but if an individual hasn't eaten for days, then that piece of meat needs to be in their stomach, not the hunter's. To solve this issue, willpower developed essential time-based features to provide balance between basic desires and long-term goals.

Employing willpower to resist urges causes negative feelings, which become increasingly uncomfortable as resistance to temptation continues over time. You will not experience specific feelings like anger, sadness or unhappiness; the feeling of willpower is more ambiguous. Participants in scientific experiments often describe willpower as frustrating or distressing, and we often frown when using willpower, a classic facial sign of negative feelings.[45, 46] You will experience this increasingly uncomfortable sensation if you place your favourite cake in front of you when you are hungry and try to continue working on your computer. These adverse feelings eventually become sufficiently strong that we succumb to temptation. In other words, using willpower to resist temptation is a progressively unpleasant experience, designed to make humans avoid sustaining it for too long. The fragility of willpower helped to maintain equilibrium between long-term benefits and satisfying immediate urges. This balance allowed humans to thrive. Willpower did not evolve to be robust and prevent us from surrendering to temptation. This would have led to everyone ignoring important basic urges that helped us survive. *Willpower was designed to break if we tried to resist temptation excessively.*

Even if willpower is successfully used to overcome one challenge, the negative sensations have implications for subsequent, seemingly unrelated situations. If the negative feelings associated with using willpower do not cause it to fracture during one instance, the same sensations will discourage its use in subsequent scenarios. In other words, using willpower once will decrease the desire to use willpower a second time. One perspective assumes that willpower is like a muscle and consumes energy when used, so there will be less energy available the next time it is required. However, this idea has been largely debunked. The reduction in willpower is not caused by a decreased *ability* to use willpower, but a reduced *willingness* to do so. Imagine putting your hand in scalding water to retrieve something. You may successfully rescue the object despite the discomfort, but you would not want to do it a second time even if you were able to. Willpower functions in the same way.

The first scientific study to investigate this idea found that people who used willpower to resist cookies quit sooner on subsequent mental tests of willpower, compared to people who did not have to resist the cookies.[47] This discovery has since been tested hundreds of times using a variety of different scenarios, including my own research with colleagues which tested participants' willpower to resist quitting a task despite physical discomfort.[48] Employing willpower to resist temptation, override instincts or persist in a task will lead to less willingness to use it again. This reduced willingness to employ willpower occurs despite the two tasks being in completely different contexts. Resisting cookies has nothing to do with subsequent mental tests, and mental tests have nothing to do with physical tests of willpower. This effect has significant implications when taken out of the psychology laboratory and into the real world. Showing dietary restraint at lunch will make it less likely that you will manage to keep your cool in a fiery work meeting. Using willpower at lunch will also make it less probable that you will be able to persuade yourself to visit the gym after work. You may resist your colleague's offer of a cake at 11am, but if you do, you will be less inclined to persist with a boring task at 11.15am. The unpleasantness of using willpower ensures that employing it again is less appealing. Given that many of us regularly encounter circumstances in which we need to show some form of restraint, it is unsurprising that diets, exercise regimes and other life changes stand little chance.

To help further protect us from neglecting our immediate basic needs, humans developed a second temporal safety mechanism. The more we resist urges over time, the more our attention intensifies on opportunities to satisfy those urges, making them increasingly desirable.[49] This process coincides with decreasing attention towards maintaining the status quo and the devaluing of long-term benefits. In our prehistoric past, whose genes thrived: the devoted soul who remained faithful to one companion, or the floozy who was tempted by beautiful counterparts? As much as I would like to say that loyalty and faithfulness won the battle for survival, the philanderer's genes were much more likely to prosper. To paraphrase Halle Berry's character, Rowena Price, in the 2007 film *Perfect Stranger*, 'Show me a beautiful person, and I'll show you a person who's tired of f**king them.' It did not benefit the human species to resist the allure of others and remain loyal to a single mate. Willpower evolved to be flimsy so that the human species would flourish. This flaw in our motivation is not reserved for pursuing food and mates. Any task or activity becomes less valuable the longer it is carried out; even the most pleasurable or exciting activities lose their appeal if undertaken excessively. At this point, our attention broadens and tempting alternatives are identified. Then, willpower does what it is designed to do.

Unfortunately, our deliberately weak willpower has been rendered inadequate by modern environments. In prehistory, temptations to satisfy urges were infrequent and often risked the wrath of the social group. Our ancestors might have encountered an occasional dilemma over whether to eat the food or not. Every now and again, they might have needed to decide whether to save energy and rest or explore new opportunities. Fast-forward to the present day and our environment has changed enormously. Food has never been so easy to obtain thanks to fast-food outlets and supermarkets. In contrast to our ancestors, our poor overwhelmed brains continually grapple with temptations.

The same can be said for any other temptations that satisfy basic urges and provide a dopamine hit. Potential mates are everywhere online, including on our phones. There is a colossal fight for our attention on social media and on our screens. Try to maintain focus on a work task, and you'll suddenly find the urge to scroll your social media feed becomes increasingly appealing. Before you know it, your willpower has snapped, and you are enthralled by Olivia's posts about her exploits in Ibiza. Willpower was designed for sporadic alternatives that were difficult, yet necessary to pursue. Now our basic urges are bombarded with opportunities to satisfy them, and our willpower is not designed to repel this level of easy, non-essential alternatives in all walks of life. We no longer need brittle willpower to nudge us towards satisfying our urges. In fact, we need resolute willpower to combat the relentlessness of modern-day temptation – but we simply do not possess it.

Compared to the experiences of our distant ancestors, modern willpower is much more sophisticated. Evolution is shifting our brains from emphasising basic urges to controlled rational judgement that allows us to focus on long-term goals and benefits. This means that the current crop of humans is better than ever at employing willpower. However, evolutionary development is infuriatingly slow. We have the tools to resist temptation, but the prefrontal cortex is still playing catch-up compared to the highly developed limbic system responsible for basic urges. The powerful cravings that evolved over thousands of generations have not disappeared. When we see a food source, especially a sweet, calorific one, the same urges are activated. When we see a person to whom we are attracted, we have not become emotionless robots who feel nothing. Our brains still douse us in dopamine. We have become better at resisting these urges through the ongoing development of our willpower, and we have created social structures like marriage and diet programmes to support us in resisting temptation, but we still have a long way to go.

All this neuroscience and evolutionary theory means that we should consider willpower to be like a tin of spaghetti hoops at the back of the cupboard. It is appropriate to reach for the can in specific situations, such as when no other food is available, or it is too late to start cooking a proper meal. In the same way, willpower can be employed during occasional motivational emergencies, like when you are exhausted or have had a super-stressful day. Willpower is also valuable in extreme circumstances, like needing to walk thirty miles to stay alive in a desert without food. But *sustained* reliance on spaghetti hoops for your nutritional needs will lead to low energy and poor health. A similar dependence on willpower as a long-term motivational source is an equally poor choice. Reaching for the spaghetti hoops should encourage a visit to the supermarket to replenish supplies with quality food alternatives. Similarly, view the need for the employment of willpower as a warning that you are using poor-quality motivation. Your goals and dreams will be unfulfilled if you do not adjust.

There is no predictable moment when willpower will break, so it is pointless trying to calculate how long temptation can be resisted. It is more useful to consider the increasing likelihood that willpower will break as time passes. The longer we resist the chocolate brownie, the more likely we are to succumb. The longer we delay going for that jog, the more likely we are to be seduced by TV. The longer we persist on the dull work task, the more boredom consumes us. Willpower is less likely to fail if you use it for one hour compared to one morning, but one minute is preferable to one hour, and one second is preferable to one minute. In this way, time is the enemy of our goals and dreams.

Willpower breaks when you need it most

Willpower is designed to be particularly fragile during specific circumstances, which makes it even more ludicrous to rely on it. When you are relaxed and have your mojo, the neural connections between your prefrontal cortex and limbic system work effectively. The two parts of the brain can communicate to ensure the more primitive aspects of the brain are kept on a leash, and reasonable decisions can be made most of the time. We may see a cake available in the office canteen, but we can resist it because a satisfying cooked meal will be waiting at home. But things change during stressful events. Reacting to stress is one of our most basic survival instincts and is mostly managed by a specific part of the limbic system. During stressful periods, hormones are released that weaken the communication channels between the prefrontal cortex and the limbic system. This snaps the leash and shifts the decision-making responsibility to the reckless limbic system, meaning that in times of stress, our thoughts, feelings and behaviour become controlled by this primitive system, which seeks to immediately satisfy urges at the expense of everything else.[50]

For our ancestors, this mechanism was effective because stress usually meant their lives were in danger and immediate survival was the only thing that mattered. But life-threatening scenarios no longer occur regularly. For us, a stressful situation is more likely to be a work project falling apart or our child having a tantrum in the shopping centre. These modern problems still cause the limbic system to dominate our decision-making, even if it is not useful. Urges that we can usually suppress when we are relaxed become too strong, so we lose our cool or indulge in junk food, alcohol, drugs, shopping or whatever vice flicks our switch. Weak willpower gets even weaker. This mechanism implies that relaxation methods like deep breathing, meditation or whatever technique you favour to help reduce stress can strengthen the communication between the different regions of the brain. They won't miraculously provide you with the resolve of a Buddhist monk, but they may help in times of motivational emergency.

In a cruel twist of fate, some people's prefrontal cortices can resume their decision-making powers after stress quicker than others. When the stressful period eases, enzymes are released to dissolve all the hormones that block the brain's communication channels. But some people are at a biological disadvantage because their enzymes are weak, so the prefrontal cortex rarely gets complete control back. This biological hindrance partly explains why some people have weaker willpower than others. This fact shouldn't be used to justify a poor lifestyle; instead, it's another reason why willpower shouldn't be relied upon to sustain lifestyle changes or achieve personal goals.

When your mojo completely vanishes and stressful episodes last for a long time, like enduring poverty or a miserable relationship, the limbic part of your brain gets so much exercise it becomes the equivalent of a super-fit athlete. Meanwhile, your prefrontal cortex gets so little exercise it becomes the slob on the sofa. This process is why impulsive behaviour can rarely be explained by biological or environmental factors on their own; it's a combination of the two. Interestingly, lead poisoning can replicate the erosion of the communication channels between your prefrontal cortex and limbic system. Next time you give in to indulgence, check that you don't have any old lead pipes leaking into your water system.

Early birds don't rely on willpower

Our vulnerable willpower is not the only way that our aims and ambitions fade over time. A more obvious threat looms larger the longer we allow time to infiltrate our lives. Understanding this danger can help protect against our human flaws.

If you are a natural scientist or science-fiction reader, you may be familiar with the remarkable Isaac Asimov. Any person who can lay claim to being one of 'The Big Three' of science-fiction writing (the others are Arthur C. Clarke and Robert A. Heinlein, in case you were wondering), having authored a three-volume tome called *Understanding Physics*, and having a crater on Mars named after them demands respect when it comes to achieving goals and creating a meaningful life. Many of the laws Asimov created to provide a structure for his fictional worlds are now used in developing artificial intelligence. In one of his famous short stories, 'The Machine that Won the War', he presents what has become known as the Asimov Corollary.

'In ten hours a day you have time to fall twice as far behind your commitments as in five hours a day.'

Put differently, giving yourself more time to achieve something is often counterproductive. The longer the delay in acting on your intentions, the greater the likelihood that unforeseen obstacles will occur. Many of us want to exercise more, for example, but struggle to sustain an active lifestyle for any meaningful period. Applying the Asimov Corollary to our daily schedule helps explain why. Imagine that you are determined to start a new healthy lifestyle. During breakfast at 7am, you develop a plan to start your new regime by going for a run at 6pm that evening. Your day is running smoothly until 2pm, when your boss calls an emergency meeting. Your company's number-one client has terminated their contract, and you are responsible for managing the account. You spend the next three hours stressing about what to do until a few colleagues suggest a visit to the local pub to commiserate. This provides an opportunity to blow off some steam and return tomorrow revitalised to start a new client-recruitment drive. Although you are still enthusiastic about your healthy lifestyle, the opportunity to be with your colleagues cannot be missed. You sink four glasses of Rioja, and the run can wait for another day.

This example will not resonate with everybody, but the idea of some unforeseen event derailing your plans will. A pipe bursts in the house, your child becomes sick at school, you trip over your partner's shoe and damage your knee. Life has countless ways of ruining your plans if you let it. The wisdom of Isaac Asimov does not just concern our exercise intentions. It applies to any planned activity, from learning a new language to reading a good book, practising origami or taking up flower arranging. Asimov's words also apply to the mundane but important tasks that we keep putting off, from fixing that puncture to sorting out a tax claim or renegotiating your phone contract. Any delay in acting on our intentions means that obstacles or alternatives are more likely as time passes. Declining willpower over time means less resistance to these stumbling blocks when they arise. Time gives a double blow to our plans, goals and intentions that leaves us with little chance of success – if we allow it.

To combat the double threat of unforeseen obstacles and the deterioration of willpower, we must recognise time as an unnecessary addition to plans and schedules that only serves to derail our goals. A preliminary step in reducing time's destructive influence is to reframe plans and goals. For example, a widespread health goal is to stop eating junk food, and a common financial ambition is to stop buying unnecessary clothes. These objectives require *continuous* avoidance of temptation. You may steer clear of junk food or frivolous purchases in the morning, but the possibility of succumbing to temptation will still be there at lunchtime, after work, in the evening and so on. As we now understand, we are designed to be weak against this type of incessant temptation, so it's not a good scenario for lifestyle changes to persist. Instead, replace 'don't' goals with 'do' goals that require action over a specific – ideally short – period.[51] A superior health goal to avoiding junk food could be to eat more fruit or vegetables for dinner. A better financial goal might be to invest money on the day that you receive your salary. These goals focus on a specific period with a clear end point (preparing dinner and payday in these examples). Rather than a never-ending assault on your willpower, the negative effects of time are limited to that brief period.

To really outwit time, a second, more potent, strategy is needed. Simply by flipping Asimov's Corollary on its head, it is possible to sidestep unnecessary reliance on willpower and reduce the likelihood of unexpected obstacles derailing your plans. Daily routines should be redesigned so that meaningful activities are completed *as soon as possible*. As mentioned in chapter two, meaningful activities are those that you *want* to do because they nourish your spirit, help you develop social relationships or allow you to progress and develop. Only when these tasks have been completed should activities that you *need* to do or *should* do be tackled. What activities will give the most satisfaction? What actions will provide a sense of accomplishment? What activities allow you to bond with others? What tasks help you get closer to your goals? Complete these personally important activities as soon as possible. Most mornings, I have a choice between learning French or opening my work email and responding to colleagues' queries. When I am on my death bed, which one of these activities will I look back on with more contentment? *Apprendre le français, bien sûr.* If I complete small chunks of personally important activities, like practising French, taking exercise and writing a book, then the day has been a success. If I leave them until my obligations are completed, then I'll be mentally depleted and willpower will be needed more often. Doing personally important activities as soon as possible also means the impact of unforeseen events is limited.

This strategy is not some bizarre request to change your morning routine to something that resembles the habits of a Silicon Valley CEO. It's merely to look at your daily routine from a different perspective and complete tasks that are meaningful in the morning, or as soon as possible. It is the total opposite to 'clearing the decks' by getting emails done or doing the laundry first before knuckling down to important stuff. This flawed strategy only allows time, and its negative implications, to obstruct your goals. The important tasks come first, the work dross or house chores come after.

To illustrate the idea of morning activity, let's rerun the day involving a work crisis with a minor change. You are determined to start a new healthy lifestyle. During breakfast at 7am, you develop a plan to go for a run during your midday lunch break. Your day is running smoothly until 2pm, when your boss calls an emergency meeting. Your number-one client has terminated their contract with you. It is fortunate that you went for a run at lunch, because the rest of the day is set to become stressful. Intentions are more likely to be fulfilled when you act on them as soon as possible. This is the case for dieting, exercising, handling work projects, managing finances, or any other context.

Of course, few people have a blank diary that allows important activities to be undertaken whenever. Work, family and social commitments often impede free time. If this is the case, don't feel obliged to take this idea to extremes and start waking up at 5am to squeeze more into your day, just because a few celebrity entrepreneurs and influencers do. The principle can still be applied even if 'as soon as possible' means mid-morning or early afternoon. Whatever the activity or change that you want to implement, act as soon as possible or risk the daily ups and downs of life obstructing your goals.

Adhering to this advice might require some creativity to reshuffle your schedule. An easy way to facilitate this principle is not to turn your work emails on, if possible. The morning is the most likely time to receive an email asking you to do something. If you are in a job where there's an expectation that emails will be responded to immediately, then, in most cases, the organisational culture needs to change – but that's a different argument (notwithstanding careers that deal with real emergencies, like nuclear reactor safety). You can also integrate the meaningful activity into other commitments. For example, a walk or some language-learning integrated into the morning commute or school run is an effective way to fulfil intentions early. It does not matter *how* you apply the idea, only that you do.

Sidestepping declining willpower and potential obstructions are not the only benefits of morning action. A handy side effect is better decision-making. Chess players need high levels of concentration to consider alternative options and make strategically important decisions. These types of decisions

are generally made in the prefrontal cortex, the same area
of the brain used for willpower. Chess is also a useful real-
world context for scientists to study, because every decision is
recorded and the consequences are quantifiable.

An analysis of millions of decisions by nearly one hundred
chess players found that, as the day progressed, players made
quicker decisions but more errors.[52] Much like our declining
willpower, the chess players employed fewer mental resources
as time wore on, resulting in poorer decision-making. If the
meaningful activities that you are trying to sustain require
complex thought, there's even more reason to complete them
in the morning. In the afternoon and evening, you've probably
spoken to a lot of people and processed a lot of information,
which requires significant mental resources, so you are less
willing to invest any more.

The analysis of chess players also evaluated their sleeping
preferences, or chronotypes. Some chess players were 'larks',
who went to bed and woke relatively early, while others were
'owls,' who were late to bed and late to rise. There was also a
middle group who were neither larks nor owls. The tendency
towards any group is partly based on individual situations (for
example, if you work as a postman, then you are likely to be a
lark) and partly based on genetics. One gene, PER3, is known
as 'the clock gene' because it helps to determine the daily cycle
of how your brain and body work. People with a relatively
lengthy PER3 gene tend to be larks and require at least seven
hours of sleep to function well. People with a shorter PER3
gene are more likely to be owls and need less sleep to function.
Unsurprisingly, the larks preferred to play chess in the morning and the owls later in the day, but this preference impacted
their decision-making. Because the larks played more morning

games, they made better decisions, whereas owls were more likely to be inaccurate. The larks had aligned with how our minds work best and benefited from it. The owls were making decisions when they shouldn't have been.

The association between natural sleep patterns and the ability to make decisions has significant implications for our lifestyles. In a survey of Italians, thirteen per cent were classified as owls (or *gufi*, in Italian), compared to nearly sixty per cent classified as larks (*allodole*).[53] The rest were neither owl nor lark. Owls were more likely to eat excessive amounts for their evening meal, and were more likely to smoke and less likely to exercise than larks. It is unsurprising that approximately fifty-five per cent of owls had heart disease, compared to only thirty per cent of larks. Similarly, around a third of owls had type 2 diabetes, compared to nine per cent of larks. Another large study found that Finnish owls (*pöllöt*) were more likely to retire early due to ill health and disability compared to larks (*kiurut*).[54] Owls are more likely to make poor lifestyle decisions that lead to illness and disease.

It's not easy being an owl, because they do not fit in with the rules of society. People often think owls are lazy because they get out of bed later, and that they are weird because they stay up late. The structure of modern society makes it more difficult for owls to make good decisions, especially regarding health. Few gyms are open late at night. It's less safe to go for a jog in the darkness. It's not easy to eat healthily if the only thing that is open is the takeaway restaurant. In Sweden, the tradition of *fika* – stopping what you're doing to have some coffee and cake, and relax and socialise – occurs at around 10am. Imagine being an owl and just getting into the office as everyone else pauses for a flat white and cinnamon bun. Societal rhythms make it very difficult for owls to be productive.

If you are a little sluggish in the morning like an owl, you may be baulking at the recommendation to do all meaningful activities as soon as possible. There's no miraculous strategy that will make you energetically leap out of bed, but there are tactics that might help ease the process. Understanding the problem and choosing the correct solution is essential. People often think they need to *wake up earlier*, so set their alarm earlier and put it next to their bed. Most often, this will lead to countless presses of the snooze button and no improvements. The real objective should not be waking up earlier but *getting out of bed earlier*. Put your alarm clock as far away from your bed as possible. The opposite corner of the bedroom is sufficient, but put in in the hallway or a different room if you can still hear it.

Now you have left the bed, the second objective is to prevent you from getting back into bed. The alarm should be near a light switch, which you need to turn on immediately. Yet even this move wouldn't stop most people from climbing straight back into bed, because it's cold outside and the bed is toasty warm. To reduce the chances of this happening, you need to make it as comfortable as you can outside the bed. It might be possible to set the heating to come on before you wake up, but this may be impractical or too expensive. Instead, make sure that you have nice warm clothes next to the alarm clock. A cosy dressing gown and snug slippers are worthy substitutes for a warm duvet. Any tactic that makes you feel as comfortable as possible removes resistance from starting the day. If you switch off the alarm but your environment remains dark and freezing, the bed will be the most appealing place in the world.

Do not suddenly try to join the 6am club if your usual wake-up is 10am. Try waking up a little earlier each week, maybe fifteen minutes at a time (see chapter seven if this is still too difficult) until you have reached your target wake-up time. Slow and steady wins the race, as a wise old tortoise once said. Don't forget to make equivalent changes to your bedtime routine, too. This might mean making some lifestyle adjustments. You might need to have dinner earlier or start watching your film a little sooner. Trying to go to bed like an owl and wake up like a lark will only lead to accumulation of fatigue.

But my gran lifts weights in the evening

There may be two issues preventing people from buying in to greater urgency for personally meaningful activities. Some people may doubt their ability to reorganise their lives in this way. A job may dictate early-morning work (are you a baker or milkman, perhaps?), young children may require packing off to nursery – and then the destruction that occurred over breakfast needs clearing up. Some lack the imagination to question their current schedule. In all these scenarios, it is *implementing* the idea that is the problem, and this should not be confused with the *effectiveness* of the idea. Former US Surgeon General C. Everett Koop handled US public health in the Ronald Reagan era. As well as pioneering several paediatric surgical techniques and generally advancing child health across the world, one of his foremost legacies is the phrase: 'Drugs don't work in patients who don't take them.' There are many effective medicines available for a wide range of conditions, but symptoms will not improve if the patient fails to take them. In fact, the World Health Organization suggest that not taking medicine is a massive, worldwide problem. In a similar vein, completing personally meaningful activities as early as possible is effective at helping you sustain them. Failure to execute this strategy means the problem lies in the individual's situation, not with the strategy. The shortcomings in our motivation and decision-making are real. When new activities are planned, the likelihood of acting on intentions decreases as the day progresses. Even when jobs, obligations or self-imposed beliefs create a barrier to morning activity, the principle can still be applied. Late afternoon is superior to the evening, but early afternoon is even better, and midday better still.

The second issue is that some people successfully sustain their hobbies and activities in the evening. This fact seems to discredit the recommendation to schedule meaningful activities as soon as possible, undermining the ideas presented in this chapter. But it doesn't. The primary reason for acting as soon as possible is to reduce the need for willpower. People with successful evening routines do not *rely* on willpower but on more effective and robust motives, like a true value or love of their pursuits. They only depend on willpower in motivational emergencies and unusual circumstances. Some people may also maintain evening or haphazard regimes using less optimal motivation, such as underlying perfectionism, compulsion or addiction. But don't be inspired by these people, as they might be maintaining an incredible work ethic while also feeling deeply unsatisfied with their accomplishments. This extreme imbalance and priority of accomplishment and progress over wellbeing has little resemblance to possessing mojo.

You may have heard the phrase: 'Choose a job you love, and you will never have to work a day in your life'. Rather than actual work, this quote refers to the *feeling* of work disappearing. Successful people who have not sacrificed their wellbeing do not employ a huge amount of mental resources to get out of bed, to grind through the mundane tasks, and to persist during difficult moments. This optimal mojo state seldom occurs overnight but develops over time. When this happens, it is possible to be more flexible in one's routine and relax the rule of urgency. How to cultivate superior motives is tackled in chapter ten of this book. People starting a life change or taking up new activities rarely possess this resilience. While these superior motives develop, the best bet to initiate and sustain positive changes in your life is to do them as soon as possible. Work or pastimes that feel like hard work will require willpower, so they need to be completed urgently – before time wreaks havoc.

In a nutshell

Implementing the ideas described in this chapter will provide initial help in regaining your mojo by helping you sustain personally meaningful hobbies, projects or lifestyle changes. In summary, willpower is not intended to do what you thought it was, and relying on it means you are heading towards frustrated ambitions and shattered dreams. Using willpower feels unpleasant and it is prone to failing, especially during times of stress. These processes helped our distant ancestors to survive, but the rapid change in our environment means they are misaligned with our current needs. In addition, the longer we delay acting on our intentions and plans, the more likely it is that life will get in the way and our goals will remain unfulfilled. To combat these weaknesses, new hobbies, meaningful activities or important changes need to be completed as soon as possible in the day. This change to routine is necessary to remove our reliance on willpower and decrease the likelihood of unforeseen obstacles.

Implementing this rule of urgency is straightforward. Think of any new goal you may have and attach a time to it. It may be to go for a run this evening, start learning a language after dinner, or start reading a book just before bed. You can even write down your work tasks, like making ten sales calls by 5pm. Now slice the timeframe in half and, if possible, in half again. Go ahead and halve it a third time, a fourth time ... you get the idea. The aim is to shave as much time off as possible to minimise the need for willpower and prevent life throwing a curve ball. Time is the enemy of your dreams.

4

Binds and beeswax

'Someone is sitting in the shade today because
someone planted a tree a long time ago.'

– Warren Buffett, successful
investor and philanthropist

There's a recent trend for fraudsters gaining celebrity status.
Shimon Hayut, also known as Simon Leviev, wooed hundreds
of women online by falsely posing as a rich, diamond-selling
entrepreneur. Thanks to Netflix, he's now more famous as
The Tinder Swindler. Anna Sorokin, also known as Anna
Delvey, conned New York's elite into thinking she was a
German heiress. She was convicted of attempted grand lar-
ceny, among other things, but a Netflix documentary and
other commercial ventures will ensure her financial comfort
for life. Elizabeth Holmes founded the biotechnology company Theranos, and was listed in *Forbes* magazine as one
of the world's most powerful women in 2015. Her company
was based on a web of lies and, in 2022, she was sentenced
to eleven years for defrauding investors. In the same year, the
actress Amanda Seyfried won an Emmy for Outstanding Lead

Actress for playing Holmes in the miniseries *The Dropout*. It seems being exceptional at lying is a sure-fire way to fame.

To sustain this level of deceit with almost everyone requires a special talent. Sorokin was born in a working-class town just outside Moscow prior to the collapse of the Soviet Union. Her father was a truck driver and her mother owned a small grocery shop. On the third day of Sorokin's trial, she refused to enter the courtroom and wept, delaying proceedings for ninety minutes. Despite her down-to-earth upbringing, her manufactured persona led to a tantrum because her outfit, which had been especially sourced for her public courtroom appearance, had not been ironed. Regardless of overwhelming evidence that Elizabeth Holmes made up details in presentations to potential investors and financial statements, her seven-day self-defence included repeated claims that she was misled by her staff and partner. These celebrity fraudsters sincerely believed that their actions were justified. In addition to lying to everyone, their special talent was incredible levels of self-delusion.

Self-deception is not new. In the New Testament's Book of Galatians, the apostle Paul explained: 'For if those who are nothing think they are something they deceive themselves.' Over three hundred years ago, in his work *Fifteen Sermons*, the philosopher Bishop Joseph Butler defined self-deception as deliberately holding contradictory beliefs. Nowadays, the Cambridge English Dictionary defines self-deceit as 'the act of hiding the truth from yourself'. Delusions take this a step further and refer to beliefs that are held despite overwhelming evidence to the contrary.

You might think that self-deceit and delusion are rare occurrences because we would know if we were lying to ourselves and put a stop to it. What is the point of trying to deceive one's own mind? Despite the absurdity of trying to tell a porky pie to ourselves, we constantly engage in this malpractice. On 1 January every year, millions convince themselves that they will be a healthier, more prudent, better version of themselves. *I will eat healthily. I will do exercise. I will save money.* This view is not simply a lie to others, it's self-deceit, because these people genuinely believe that this will be the case. When people reflect on an argument, each person often vigorously holds on to a wholly different view of what happened. If objective facts of the argument don't align with our perspective, we can easily distort the facts and sustain our own view. Most of the time, we are not aware that this self-delusion occurs. Victims of abusive relationships often self-deceive by neglecting to admit the damage being done. People with clinical disorders often delude themselves by rejecting the idea that they are ill. Individuals with narcissistic personality disorder create a cycle of self-delusion by distorting events to fit their own reality, which strengthens their beliefs and leads to further distortion. Inside and outside of clinical settings, self-deceit is incredibly common.

Why we self-deceive

Self-deceit is so prevalent because it provides many benefits. Its major function is to protect the individual's ego and sense of worth by justifying dubious or immoral acts. For example, people will often justify aggression and violence by distorting the truth and believing that the victim deserved it. Self-deceit is also used to justify cheating. In a series of scientific experiments, participants were given an intelligence test, but some were given the opportunity to cheat and see the answers.[55] Despite this advantage, the cheaters attributed their success on the test to their intelligence rather than the more obvious reason of having seen the answers beforehand. They also expected to perform similarly well on a subsequent test, even though they would not be able to see the answers. Even when researchers offered up to twenty dollars to accurately predict their score on a second test, the cheaters were still overoptimistic. Their self-deception was so ingrained that a cash incentive couldn't stop them doing it. The renowned psychologist Carl Jung described a 'shadow' of unacceptable characteristics that we all possess but hide from ourselves. Many of us are unable to accept our own aggressiveness, dishonesty, selfishness, greed, jealousy and so on. Psychotherapy can be a very disturbing experience for some people because this self-deception is eroded, and individuals are made aware of these unwanted traits.

As the celebrity tricksters described previously showed, self-deceit can also make it easier to get others to believe falsehoods. Self-deception gives us confidence in what we are saying, which makes us more persuasive and means that other people are more likely to believe it too. In another experiment, participants who knew that they would be required to convince others of their high intelligence rated themselves as more intelligent, compared to participants who were not told about the impending persuasion task.[56] In other words, the individuals who knew that they needed to persuade others inflated their perceived intelligence beforehand. What's more, this false confidence worked, and the panel of people were more likely to believe the overconfident participants. The need to protect one's ego and convince others are characteristics shared by many. Politicians vehemently justified their drinks parties during Covid-19 pandemic lockdowns. Bankers who caused the 2008 global financial meltdown truly believed that their actions were justified. Your financial adviser will be adamant that their advice is in your best interests, and financial incentives for selling that product have not swayed their recommendations. Examples like these often do not include a malicious intent to deceive. It's more likely that they have convinced themselves that their actions are warranted, which makes it easier to convince others.

Similar effects can be seen in famous people. When the cyclist Lance Armstrong had to defend himself against media accusations of doping, he often reacted with cast-iron confidence and venom. This level of response would be difficult if he didn't believe in what he was saying. We are currently in the grasp of arguably the greatest self-deceiver of all time. In 2017, twenty-seven essays from distinguished psychiatrists and psychologists were collated about one person. These essays speculated that the individual was symptomatic of many different illnesses and disorders that contain self-delusion as a symptom, such as narcissism, antisocial personality and dementia. The collection of essays is titled *The Dangerous Case of Donald Trump*.[57] Despite these disturbing appraisals, Trump convinced enough people to drive him all the way to the White House (and, at the time of writing, has just done so again). In fact, seekers of social status are especially prone to self-deception. Falsely inflating their own confidence and esteem acts as a protection mechanism, especially when their ego is under threat.

Another reason we self-deceive is because we are abysmal

at appreciating and predicting the future. When we consider an event or decision in the future, rather than in the moment, we become increasingly inaccurate and self-deluded. For example, do you think you will be restrained rather than indulgent when it comes to snacking next week? A sneaky study by psychologists sought to find the answer to this question.[58] Researchers visited the workplace of around two hundred people employed in various industries, such as banking, healthcare and education. They told employees that they would be returning in one week's time with a variety of snacks, but the workers had to pre-order their choices now. The choices could be broadly separated into healthy snacks, like fruit, and unhealthy treats, like chocolate bars. Eighty-six people chose a healthy snack.

As promised, the researchers returned a week later with the snacks. However, the sly researchers pretended that they had lost the participants' pre-orders, but said this didn't matter because they had plenty of each snack available. They even elaborately 'proved' their mistake by showing the participants a list containing only their names and no choice. In truth, the researchers hadn't lost the initial choices at all. They just wanted to see if people changed their minds.

When snack time came, only thirty-four people chose a healthy snack. Over sixty per cent of the self-proclaimed healthy eaters had deluded themselves into thinking they would want a healthy snack but then took a treat.

This self-deception doesn't only occur when asking about eating habits. If you ask people to choose a film to watch in one or two weeks' time, people often select a highbrow film like *Oppenheimer*. When it comes to the film night, a significant percentage of people will change their minds and choose an easy watch, like *Barbie*.[59] Are people deliberately and maliciously lying to researchers and themselves? Of course not. They are simply deceiving themselves because they fail to consider what is likely to happen or how they will feel in the future.

We can see this phenomenon derail our best intentions in all parts of life. Many individuals make a pact with themselves and others to quit smoking or drinking. Promises like these are not lies, but they are often delusional because the person has failed to consider what is very likely to occur in the future. For example, they may have underestimated the potent urge for a nicotine hit, or how bored they will be on Tuesday evening without a can of German Pilsner. Fast-food giants spend billions teasing your saintly intentions by advertising healthy salads and low-calorie options. But they understand that your immediate desires will dominate when you arrive in the restaurant, and you will likely leave with a triple cheeseburger and extra-large milkshake. You did not want to fit into your swimwear anyway. Are you going to wisely save a chunk of your earnings next month? You will think the answer is yes, because you haven't considered the lure of those fabulous new trainers that keep popping up in your adverts.

Delusions caused by failing to consider the future occur in organisations too. In the 2010 UK election campaign, the Liberal Democrats famously pledged not to raise university tuition fees. This promise was made despite it being highly improbable that the Liberal Democrats would win the general election outright. Their only route to power was in coalition with one of two larger parties who strongly favoured raising tuition fees. The Liberal Democrats had little chance of fixing university tuition fees and they had to go back on their promise once they were in coalition with the Conservatives, but they deceived themselves into thinking they could.

Governments often similarly claim that they will spend billions to benefit public health in their election manifestos, only to row back on their promises because of supposedly unforeseen circumstances, like war. If only they'd considered the fact that global peace has *never* occurred. Even in the relative calm of Europe, the period of peace before Russia's invasion of Ukraine was the longest we'd ever had. Conflict was very likely to occur sooner rather than later. Every year, there is a one in fifty chance of a pandemic with no immediate cure or vaccine.[60] To put these odds in perspective, three horses with longer odds have won the Grand National in the last fourteen years. Governments should have been at least partially ready for such an event, not living in a state of delusion because they didn't consider likely events in the future. A business may plan a costly expansion programme, but fail to consider that, since 1857, a financial recession has hit the United States (and very often, therefore, global trade) every three years, on average.[61] In all walks of life, from personal choices to global decision-making, our inability to predict the future despite overwhelming evidence savages the best-laid plans.

It is arguable that choosing a chocolate bar over a healthy piece of fruit, or a comedy over a movie about mass destruction, is a sensible choice. However, our lack of consideration for the future also encourages completely illogical decisions. If someone offered you £10 or £20 now, you would be very likely to take the latter. However, if someone offered you £10 now or £20 next week, you would be much more likely to take the smaller cash reward.[62] We are inclined towards immediate rewards even if the delayed reward is greater, because we significantly overestimate the risk of waiting for the benefit. The human brain has evolved in this way to help us survive. For our distant predecessors, a decision whether to stop and eat a small bounty now or continue to see if a bigger prize could be discovered would be weighted towards the first option, because survival was paramount. In pre-history, it was too risky to gamble on things that might not occur in the future, even if they would be more beneficial in the longer run.

Our brains still work like this nowadays. We think that something might occur in the future that would prevent us from receiving the £20, despite the actual risk of this happening being very low. Humans value immediate outcomes much more than delayed outcomes, even if the delayed outcome is a better option, because we're awful at evaluating the future. In a similar way, it is often a mistake to buy cheaper products and continually replace them because doing so is more expensive in the long run, compared to buying costlier products that last many years. Yet this is what many people prefer, because they do not accurately evaluate the long-term picture. Rarely does it pay dividends to pay a certain amount per month for your mobile phone. Paying for it outright often works out much cheaper, but few people take this option.

It is often wise to save some spare money for big life purchases that occur later in life, such as buying a house, sending your children to university, or that circumnavigation of the world you have always dreamed about. Nonetheless, we have an inability to predict our desires for a big night out, a meal at a fancy restaurant, or the natty suit that will only be worn once. As a result, many people tend to find it difficult to save money even if they have the resources to do so. Some people

are more prone to this effect than others. Those who are
socio-economically disadvantaged tend to have a powerful
present-focused self and are more likely to go against their
well-meaning long-term intentions.[63] A vicious cycle develops
in which the underprivileged are not able to invest in the long
term, which exaggerates their socio-economic disadvantage.
This pattern does not just concern financial investment, but
investment in health, education and so on.

Our inability to consider the future also leads us to self-
deceive by lavishly underestimating the duration of tasks and
projects. Nowhere is this better illustrated than the construction industry. Take the most-visited site in Spain, the iconic
church the Sagrada Família in Barcelona. The UNESCO
world heritage site is undoubtably a wondrous piece of archi-
tecture, but its bizarre history is what makes it so popular.
The building project began in 1882. Chief architect and leader
in Catalan modernism Antoni Gaudí dedicated his whole life
to the project. At the time of his death in 1926, less than a
quarter of the basilica was complete. Progress remained slow
in subsequent years, largely because civil wars tend to dry up
public funding for building projects. The Sagrada Família
remains the largest unfinished Roman Catholic church in the
world. Imagine setting out on a project and underestimating
how long it would take by over a century. Not that Gaudí
is bothered, but it's due to be completed in 2026, a century
after he died.

In Germany, you can buy a board game called *Das
Verrückte Flughafenspiel*, 'The Crazy Airport Game'. Created
by Berliners Philipp Messinger and Bastian Ignaszewski,
the aim of the game is to squander as many taxpayer euros
as possible while building an airport. This may seem like a

niche topic on which to base a board game, but it was developed as a satirical response to the real construction of Berlin Brandenburg Airport. The flagship airport was scheduled to be completed in 2011, but the airport's managing company announced that the opening date would be postponed to June 2012. Then, in May 2012, the managing company postponed the opening again. The new opening date was 17 March 2013, which was subsequently pushed to 27 October 2013. This opening was postponed again at the beginning of 2014. Over the next few years, several catastrophes followed, including escalators that were too short, engineers faking their credentials. At the beginning of 2017, the managing company sensibly confirmed that the airport would open at an unspecified date. After a decade of overly optimistic deadlines, the airport became a national joke, but it finally opened in 2020 to great fanfare and amusement.

The Sagrada Família and Berlin Airport may be famous examples of underestimating the time required to complete projects, but they are not rare occurrences. Anyone who has had some building work carried out on their house knows what this feels like. Delayed construction projects fail to account for a fundamental principle of planning. In the 1970s and 1980s, computer scientists frequently debated when a computer programme would be able to beat a grandmaster chess player. A leader in this field, Douglas Hofstadter, observed that people thought it would take a decade, only for a decade to pass and software programmes to still not be even close to this level. This was an extreme example of Parkinson's law, as described in chapter two, only the time-scale was a guideline rather than a strict deadline, so the task duration continued to expand (IBM's Deep Blue computer system finally beat Garry Kasparov over six games in 1997). This error in judgement became known as Hofstadter's Law:

> 'It always takes longer than you expect, even when you take into account Hofstadter's Law.'

Odysseus and the Sirens

Solving our tendency to underestimate the time required for tasks is straightforward once we know why we do it. The major factor causing us to claim we can do something in six weeks, despite all the evidence suggesting it will take ten weeks, is ego. We make overly ambitious claims because we want to portray the ideal version of ourselves, not the real version who struggles to stay motivated and makes mistakes. To remove the effect of ego on our predictions, we should think about how long it will take *others* to complete a task, rather than ourselves. We do not typically view others in such a positive light, so we can account for their predictable flaws more easily. The other people we think about don't need to be specific, but they do need to possess similar skills and attributes to you. If you are planning to open your first restaurant, do not estimate how long it would take Jamie Oliver to achieve such a feat, because he already has extensive experience in realising this ambition. Considering how long a project would take someone with a similar skill set will remove the influence of our own vanity.

To solve the other types of self-deception, such as changing our decisions and reneging on plans, we need an alternative solution. The *Odyssey* is the Greek mythological sequel to Homer's *Iliad*. A huge poem split into twenty-four books and written around 2,700 years ago, the *Odyssey* is widely considered one of the most enduring narratives still read by modern audiences. If you are not familiar with this literary heavyweight, the *Odyssey* follows the Greek hero Odysseus on his ten-year voyage home to Ithaca after the Trojan War. His crew perish as they confront numerous deadly challenges. Back at home, Odysseus is assumed dead, and his wife, Penelope, fends off admirers desperate for her hand in marriage. The outlook is bleak for our hero, but I won't spoil the ending.

The influence of Odysseus' voyage can still be observed today. The phrase 'the lesser of two evils', for example, originates from Odysseus' dilemma when he had to choose between sailing near Scylla, a six-headed sea monster, and Charybdis, a dangerous whirlpool, as he navigated the narrow Strait of Messina. Adaptations of the one-eyed cyclops, Polyphemus, have since appeared in several Hollywood tales, such as *Clash of the Titans* and *X-Men*. Perhaps the most famous episode in the narrative, however, is Odysseus' encounter with the Sirens in book twelve. In Homer's tome, the Sirens were ugly beasts who lived in a meadow, but they have been more generally represented as beautiful creatures from the sea. The Sirens would torment sailors by seducing them with beautiful voices and songs, enticing them to sail too close to treacherous rocks where they would meet their doom.

Fortunately, Odysseus was tipped off about the Sirens by the goddess Circe, and put in place some cunning strategies to combat the singers' allure. Odysseus craftily instructed his crew to plug their ears with beeswax so they could not hear the Sirens' mesmeric tones. Odysseus himself adopted an extreme tactic and had his crew bind him to the mast of the ship so he was physically restrained. When the ship encountered the Sirens, their song was so seductive that Odysseus begged to be released from his binds, but his loyal men only bound him tighter. These tactics were effective, and the crew sailed past the island of the Sirens and lived to fight another day.

This mythological saga about binds and beeswax tells us what we can do if we recognise our flaws, just like Odysseus did. We need to acknowledge that our future environments will be imperfect and contain many obstacles impeding our path. We will very likely be in a different mental state than we were when the plan was made. This self-awareness allows us to create binding Odysseus-style contracts that can withstand these shortcomings. Odysseus and his crew knew that they needed to sail past the irresistible Sirens, so he planned accordingly. In the same way, you know that obstacles are coming, and you will probably be tired and stressed when they do. The cake that will ruin your beach body will come. The night out that will ruin your finances will come. We all have our own personal Sirens that will tempt us.

A good friend of mine employed an Odysseus-style contract to avoid pints of lager in favour of low-calorie gin and slimline tonics. On a night out with his friends, he knows that most will be drinking pints, and it will be tempting to similarly imbibe satisfying – but calorific and hangover-inducing – lager. To combat this temptation, he uses a rather unique contract. His political preference leans to the left and he despises anything to the right. And so, if he succumbs to drinking a pint, he has instructed his wife to donate £100 from his personal account to the coffers of a right-leaning political party. If he drinks lager, he is bolstering the war chest of a political party he loathes. Quirky but effective. He doesn't drink lager.

It is not necessary to be as creative as my friend with your Odysseus contracts. Want to go for a run next week? Arrange to meet a friend to run with you, because it is difficult to bail out when your bestie is waiting on a street corner. Signing up for an activity and paying for it in advance also makes a great Odysseus contract, because most people dislike wasting money by not attending. Broadcasting to other people what you are setting out to achieve is also a useful bind, because this acts as a social contract. Not wanting to back out of a commitment made to friends is an effective motivator, and good friends should support you in trying to accomplish your goal. Setting up your bank accounts to automatically save or invest money makes it difficult for your present-focused self to back out on a plan to save more. There are thousands of ways in which you can compel yourself to act in your future self-interest. Odysseus' legacy tells us how to overcome the effects of time by compelling us to stick to our plans. Your present-focused self is flaky, so make binds and contracts that force you to stick to your noble intentions.

The creativity of Boris Johnson

Odysseus contracts build a coercive bridge between your present-focused and future-focused selves. If you don't fulfil your intentions, you'll let your friends down, you'll be £100 worse off, or whatever deterrent you chose. However, a more ideal scenario is for your two selves to be like twins, rather than strangers, so each knows exactly what the other will think and do. Advertising companies are excellent at linking present- and future-focused selves. Adverts about retirement and funeral planning often employ actors who are considerably younger than their supposed age. This approach paints a picture of the future, older self closely resembling the present self for the target demographic, which makes planning ahead more likely and increases the chances of the viewer purchasing the product. Greater continuity between your present-focused and future-focused selves means that you will be more likely to adhere to long-term goals and less likely to change your mind. Additionally, your future-focused self might not set such unrealistic expectations of your present-focused self.

To enhance the relationship between our present-focused and future-focused selves, we can turn to the world of politics and, specifically, the touchy subject of Brexit. In 2015, Boris Johnson stated that withdrawing from the European Union (EU) was a valid option, but not his preference. In early 2016, he was still undecided which way to vote. When interviewed, he suggested it was in Britain's interest to be 'intimately engaged' with the EU, and that Brexit would undoubtably lead to business upheaval.

Johnson's flirtation with remaining in the EU is now infamous, so how did he finally decide and become the figurehead of the Brexit campaign? He wrote two draft newspaper columns, one outlining his recommendation to remain in the EU, the other backing Brexit. The latter was published in the *Telegraph* on 21 February 2016, but the other one was leaked to the *Sunday Times* a few days later. In the Remain version, Johnson wrote of the benefits of being pro-EU, including meaningful global relationships and the advantages gained by the rest of the world. The costs of EU membership were a small price to pay for these benefits. He downplayed any problems concerning sovereignty if we remained, and backed the then-prime minister David Cameron and his pragmatic deal with the EU.

Boris Johnson claims he wrote this 'semi-parodic' Remain article as a mental exercise to help him decide which way to lean. He wrote both articles to peer into the future and observe how he felt about each choice. Johnson has had to defend this mental exercise staunchly, and opponents accused him of dishonesty. I suspect that if he wasn't such a controversial figure in the public eye, the exercise would be viewed as an innovative way of deliberating on an important decision. By acting out both alternatives, he made it possible to judge what he would think and feel in the future. He was connecting his present-focused and future-focused selves to allow them to come to a mutually agreeable decision.

You don't have to write a news article outlining different perspectives you could take; just a little foresight is necessary. Successful businesses often engage in horizon-scanning, where they try to anticipate future risks and opportunities to help build resilience. Your personal life can benefit from horizon-scanning too. When planning a new diet, for example, imagine getting home from your difficult job and sitting at the dinner table with a carrot smoothie and a cracker. It's very likely that your present-focused self will demand a more satisfying meal, so plan accordingly. Some forward-thinking firms insert people on interview panels whose role is to be a pain in the neck and vouch for a different candidate than the one other panel members want to hire. Likewise, your present-focused self often has different, annoying, but equally valid opinions that need considering when making plans. You might fancy cooking a delicious Sri Lankan beef curry worthy of an Instagram post next Tuesday evening. A conversation with your annoying present-focused self, however, might reveal that you will not have the energy to prepare and cook food for three hours when the time comes, so a simpler alternative meal might be warranted.

In a nutshell

We are terrible at predicting what will happen and how we will feel in the future. These flaws are intensified by a tendency to undervalue benefits that are accrued in the future. To make matters even worse, we grossly underestimate the time it will take us to complete projects and reach our goals. All these failings add up to a life of unfulfilled intentions, derailed plans and misplaced mojo. But we don't have to accept this outcome. When planning how long activities take, judge how long it will take others to finish them. This approach removes your ego from decision-making and enhances accuracy. The Greek hero Odysseus knew that he would be fatally tempted by the allure of the Sirens, so he put aids in place to help him stick to his plan. You should do the same by making it difficult to default on your plans and intentions. Recruit friends, set up penalties, pay up front and tell everyone about your plans to help you fulfil them. Finally, take a leaf out of Boris Johnson's book and develop the relationship between your present-focused and future-focused self. Horizon-scan to include your present-focused self in decisions about lifestyle changes and new projects.

5

Mind the gap

'Nobody can whistle a symphony.'

– Halford E. Luccock, minister and Yale professor

The New York thoroughfare Madison Avenue may have entered wider public awareness thanks to Don Draper and the TV series *Mad Men*, but it's been the spiritual home of US advertising firms for a century. During the 1960s, corporate organisations began to realise that following the advertising rules was a flawed business strategy and they started looking for something different. Arguably the person who most signified this change of approach was legend of Madison Avenue and native New Yorker Peretz Rosenbaum. Even at the start of his career, Rosenbaum knew the importance of effective branding. He changed his name to Paul Rand and became one of the most famous designers of the last century.

What set Rand apart from his peers was his ability to eschew traditional US design standards and to take inspiration from European artistic principles from earlier in the century. As the Cold War escalated, the US government and businesses were also quick to promote Rand's abstract art because it was seen as the antithesis to formulaic communist art. His application of German creative principles can be seen in Rand's most famous contribution to corporate design: the IBM logo he created in 1972. IBM's graphics had been largely unchanged since World War I, and each of their advertising campaigns was completely unconnected with the preceding campaign. With Rand's input, IBM changed to rely on a whole new field of corporate identity instead of solely relying on advertising. IBM's new identity became instantly recognisable around the world. Everything from their stationery to their buildings had the same modern logo. Rand created an emblem consisting of a collection of horizontal bars in eight rows, but the human brain perceives these shapes as forming three letters: I, B, M.

Inspired by Rand's work, graphic designers across the world now play with the space between words and images to make smaller objects into a larger theme. Unilever's motif includes several individual icons representing the company's commitment to sustainable living (some environmental activists may have choked on these words, but that debate is for another time). These include a sun, a dove, a plant, a spark and other symbols that represent the company's ethos. But when we view their logo, we do not typically see these individual shapes, we merely observe a big, blue letter 'U'. It is not by chance that logos like IBM and Unilever's are so appealing to the human eye.

How many stars make up a constellation?

In the early twentieth century, German-educated psychologists Max Wertheimer, Kurt Koffka, and Wolfgang Köhler studied how the human mind interprets what we see. At the time, scientists assumed that people perceive individual objects in isolation, even if there are several objects in the person's vision. For example, they believed that individuals would see a house, a garden and a garage separately, rather than viewing them collectively as a home. Human perception and real experience were not investigated because they were considered unscientific. But Wertheimer and colleagues noticed that this approach made it difficult to explain something called the *phi* effect. When light bulbs are placed in a line and illuminated rapidly one after the other, it gives the impression that the light is moving. This perception means that we do not observe each light bulb in isolation, but consider the previous and subsequent light bulbs too. Wertheimer proposed that how humans perceive an object depends on its relationship with other objects. This discovery led to the creation of the Law of Prägnanz (German for 'conciseness'), which explains that the brain chooses to see a set of objects in the easiest way possible. Unlike previous thinking, humans do typically perceive a home, rather than the individual house, garden and garage. This breakthrough and many more of the psychologists' discoveries became known as Gestalt principles (*gestalt* is German for 'shape' or 'form'), and they became one of the most influential scientific theories of the twentieth century. Indeed, Koffka coined the phrase, 'The whole is something else [not 'greater', as is often thought] than the sum of its parts.'

Much of the work of Paul Rand and his contemporaries, including the logo of IBM and many others, is so appealing because it aligns with the Gestalt principles discovered decades earlier. In particular, the Gestalt rule of proximity describes how the human brain often perceives multiple objects as one larger object if they are physically close to each other. The human brain attempts to simplify and organise structures that consist of many components, because it is more efficient to visualise one combined item than several individual pieces. Millions of stars randomly reside in the sky, yet humans have decided that constellations exist, so we see the Plough, the Bear, the Libran Scales, and many other fictitious astrological arrangements. German design principles were underpinned by German science.

Examples of the spatial proximity principle can be found everywhere. When you drive, your brain doesn't perceive every single car in isolation but provides an overview of how busy the road is in front of you. People don't complete jigsaw puzzles by considering each piece in isolation; they consider each piece in relation to other pieces and the overall picture. Supermarkets also use spatial proximity to make you spend money. The tortilla chips, salsa and guacamole are typically next to each other because marketing executives want you to perceive all three products as a collective. We might only intend to buy some chips, but end up purchasing a Mexican banquet. Spatial proximity partly explains why celebrities are used to endorse products. Having a pop star, athlete or movie icon standing with a product creates a relationship between the two. David Beckham next to a whisky bottle, George Clooney with an espresso, Lewis Hamilton hastily putting on a Swiss watch on the podium for the cameras. We don't perceive the celebrity and object in isolation but merge them into a bigger composite, which often reflects a lifestyle that many individuals desire. People are more likely to buy products that are endorsed by a celebrity, and make faster choices to do so, compared to products without celebrity backing.[64]

Children know best

Several decades after spatial proximity was first proposed, scientists explored the idea of proximity applied to objects and events over time. Temporal proximity means that objects that have small intervals of time between them tend to be perceived as a whole, just like the lines in the IBM logo. Only recently have we begun to understand that this idea can be applied to our actions and goals to help us maintain a fulfilling lifestyle. The proximity principle does not only apply to our vision, but it also applies to our motivation.[65]

The phrase 'a means to an end' was first recorded in the seventeenth century to describe a situation in which necessary but unrewarding steps are taken in pursuit of a desired goal. Adult life is dominated by this outlook. Run to get fit, work to earn money, diet to look good, go to college to get a better job. This attitude appears to be a sensible one, because acting without a motivating reason could be seen as a waste of time. In contrast, young children are not ruled by this mantra. Children act for action's sake. For these innocent youngsters, the means *is* the end. Ask a three-year-old why they manically run the length of the kitchen. The answer will not be fitness or urgency. In fact, the question does not make sense. They run to run. It is easy to assume that adults have the more beneficial approach because they understand that the rigours of life demand a goal-driven perspective. However, the opposite is true. When it comes to goals and their motivational significance, young children have a more effective viewpoint than adults.

Unknowingly, young children apply the rule of temporal proximity by perceiving their actions and goals as one thing occurring at the same time. They play for the sake of playing and explore for the sake of exploring. In contrast, adults have allowed time to separate our actions and goals, so we tend to view them independently. We go for a run to be healthy in the future. We work to get our pay cheque at the end of the month. This temporal separation makes our motivation for activities weak because we are generally energised by the outcome, not the action. We feel motivated at the thought of losing weight, not by the prospect of dieting. We are motivated by the prospect of holidaying in the Maldives, not by the need to save money to afford it. Significant time gaps between action and outcome prevent the motivational power of the outcome transferring to the action. This is not the case in children, where time has not invaded the relationship between action and goal, so they remain tightly bonded. As they develop, children have this purer perspective forced out by societal pressures (adults) until they conform to an inferior 'means to an end' approach. The desire to cook a beautifully constructed meal should stem from the pure joy of executing a culinary magnum opus, not wanting to share it on social media and receive 'likes' several hours later.

To recover our childhood outlook, our actions and goals require temporal proximity, rather than the spatial proximity employed by the world's best designers. We need to remove time by prioritising an outcome, benefit or reward that occurs as close to the action as possible. Ask lifelong exercisers why they exercise, for example, and most will name an immediate outcome, such as pleasure. In contrast, most people who fail to sustain exercise regimes were likely motivated by delayed outcomes, such as weight loss. People find it easier to maintain activities when they focus on relatively instant outcomes or rewards, compared to delayed outcomes.

This effect is not limited to helping us maintain exercise regimes. Scientific evidence demonstrates that people are better at sticking to New Year's resolutions, children are better at studying and people eat more vegetables if they focus on immediate outcomes, rather than delayed outcomes.[66] In fact, this principle can be applied to a variety of other contexts. If work bonuses are already part of an organisational culture, they should be paid immediately after the work is completed to motivate employees to a greater extent, rather than at the end of the financial year (although see below for the dangers of using external rewards to motivate). Organisations could save millions yet maintain employee motivation by providing smaller but immediate financial incentives compared to whopping bonuses once a year. If you are aiming to start a new business venture or side hustle, the worst thing you can focus on is getting rich in several years' time to stay motivated. It's nice to have this dream in the back of your mind, but you need immediate rewards to motivate you daily. The satisfaction of learning a new business skill or the achievement of making a new contact are much better outcomes to focus on to keep you moving towards the larger ambition.

Children will also read more in class if they know that the sticker (or whatever reward may be offered) is given immediately, rather than at the end of the class. Immediate rewards do not have to be tangible – they can include simple pleasures like enjoyment, enhanced mood and other psychological benefits. Indeed, exercising for mental benefits rather than other reasons might help beginners stick to their lifestyle changes more successfully, because these benefits are often experienced instantly. In contrast, physical health benefits are often delayed. Social benefits are also an effective and immediate gain from many activities, but are not always essential. People often read, run or create on their own in order to relax, experience solitude or focus. These are great immediate rewards too. In any context, the activity and outcome, or the means and the end, need to be as temporally inseparable as possible.

Some immediate benefits provide a greater motivational boost than others. If you are lucky enough to have discovered an activity with an immediate *internal* benefit for you, like love and enjoyment, then do not let society or your brain ruin it by adding an external incentive. Hundreds of scientific studies demonstrate that adding an external incentive, such as a monetary reward, when superior internal motives already exist can reduce engagement in the long run, especially if that external incentive is then removed.[67] Our sex lives provide a real-life example of the dangers of adding external incentives unnecessarily. In the beginning of most relationships, we have sex for internal rewards, like orgasms, pleasure, intimacy or connection. These are great motivators to encourage further sex. Nonetheless, for many adult couples, there may come a time when starting a family comes on the agenda. Suddenly, sex becomes about creating a baby. If you are lucky, conception occurs quickly, but if not, then the means (having sex) to an end (a baby) approach begins to dominate. Sex becomes about an external benefit (having a baby), and the internal benefits are ignored. This perspective makes it very difficult to re-engage in sex after childbirth, even when the nappy changing and sleepless nights have receded. The power of keeping the immediate benefits of sex (and any other activity) at the forefront of your mind cannot be underestimated.

External incentives are often used because many think that other people prefer them, even though they personally prefer internal motives. In a scientific experiment, young children rated crackers as less tasty and consumed fewer of them when they were told that it would make them healthy (a common extrinsic reason for consuming food), compared to when they were given no information about the crackers.[68] This same effect occurred when researchers suggested that crackers would help the children to read and count. If food is tasty, then let this be the reward. This same principle can be applied to numerous scenarios. If your employees don't receive financial bonuses but still enjoy their work, don't start giving them bonuses. If your child gets satisfaction out of tidying their toys away, then do not introduce treats for doing so. If your students love learning, then leave them be. In any context, do not provide an immediate external incentive, reason or motivation when an immediate internal incentive already exists.

The drugs do work

The influence of our bias for immediate outcomes should not be underestimated. For example, it is shaping entire health-care systems, and arguably not in a good way. Obesity is one of the greatest public health challenges of the twenty-first century. At least 2.8 million adults die each year globally because of being overweight or obese. In countries such as the UK and the US, obesity is one of the leading causes of preventable death. Tackling obesity can reduce the likelihood of some cancers, type 2 diabetes and various heart problems. It's no wonder that losing weight is often cited as the most common New Year's resolution. Whether we like it or not, many of us need to lose a few pounds for better health. Governments across the world are playing their part by funding major research programmes to find the solution. But there's a problem with where this is leading.

At the end of the twentieth century, obesity was largely considered as a *condition* resulting from consistently poor lifestyle choices. Eating healthier and being more physically active were considered two of the best ways to tackle obesity – or, less dramatically, to fit into your old jeans. The problem is that these healthy habits are very difficult to sustain, because they are not *immediately* rewarding for most people. Eating a salad in a restaurant, especially when your fellow diners are indulging in a gourmet burger, is not immediately rewarding for many of us. Other factors compound the issue, like convenience food being less time-consuming to prepare but lower quality than fresh food. In many housing areas, the nearest shops are over a mile away, so it is inconvenient to walk or cycle. These are just a few of the difficulties in promoting a healthy lifestyle, which meant that politicians and policy makers started looking for another, more successful way for people to lose weight.

How obesity was viewed fundamentally changed in the early twenty-first century. In 2004, respected scientist Professor George Bray detailed how obesity meets all the criteria to be called a *disease*. Around the same time, future Dean of the Harvard Medical School Professor Jeffrey S. Flier suggested that effective medication for obesity needed to be sought. Authoritative voices like these swayed most clinical bodies to redefine obesity as a disease. To most people, the change from condition to disease might not mean much, but it has huge ramifications for all of us. Defining obesity as a disease meant it became medicalised, and was now the responsibility of clinicians to treat, manage and cure.[69] This perspective has many benefits, such as an acknowledgement that some causes of obesity are outside people's control. It also has one unfortunate drawback. The classification of obesity as a disease justifies treating it with drugs, which enabled the big pharmaceutical companies to focus their research and development – and, more significantly, their marketing and sales departments – on preventing obesity.

Weight-loss drugs are big news. Semaglutide drugs like Wegovy and Ozempic significantly reduce obesity and are already being hailed as miracle drugs. The benefits of drugs like these are rapid. When you receive the injection, within minutes your appetite will reduce. You will eat less. Within a day or two, the pounds will begin to fall off without you having to budge off the sofa. Traditional diets often rely on your determination not to eat certain things despite craving them. Physical activity is hard work and has no immediate weight-loss reductions. The weight-loss drugs benefit from the human bias that means relatively instant benefits are more motivating than delayed benefits. If everyone is given a choice between taking a drug or pounding the streets for three months and eating salad, guess which one will be the more popular choice?

The weight-loss pharmaceutical market is forecasted to grow by $54 billion by 2030. Herein lies the problem. The pharmaceutical industry is not going to advocate for life-style changes to solve the obesity crisis. It's going to market its drugs, because it wants to make a profit. This policy means that it will become very expensive to treat obesity, especially compared to the cost of going for a walk. Wegovy costs the NHS £175.80 per 2.4mg pack, but this doesn't include the costs of prescribing, delivering, clinical support and all the other processes that lead to you injecting a dose. Financially stricken healthcare systems will fall deeper into economic crisis. Humans are not biased towards financially sensible options; we are biased towards immediately reward-ing options.

And what happens when the prescription stops? It is recom-mended that weight-loss drugs are complemented by lifestyle advice to help keep the weight off, but this doesn't work in the long term. We know this because scientists have been trying this educational strategy for over fifty years without success. Most people will make no long-term lifestyle changes, but simply rely on the drug to do its work because it's immedi-ately rewarding. When the drugs stop, weight will be regained because the daily habits and routines to keep the weight off for life have not been implemented. Most people will go back to square one. Taking weight-loss medication will be effective in the short term because the benefits are almost instant. But it will only delay the need to make significant lifestyle changes; it will not remove this need.

This example is just one of many ways in which our preference for immediate rewards covertly influences our actions – yet we can consciously take advantage of this. To put this immediacy principle into practice, ask yourself why you want to start a new activity, project or lifestyle change.

If it's for some outcome that appears much later than when the activity is carried out, then you are setting yourself up to fail. Find a new motivation if you can. Mental and social benefits are a good place to start. If you can't find an immediate reward from the activity that you want to start, are you considering the right activity for you? It is common, especially in January, to see people running around the streets looking in a terrible mess: breathing so heavily that it looks like they're having a panic attack, face about to explode, clenched fists pumping the air to reach the next lamp post. There are no immediate benefits to taking this approach, so the likelihood of them still running in February is low. Have you ever seen experienced recreational runners do this? No; they look like they are floating along the pavement without a care in the world. An analysis of over 14,000 runners showed that faster runners trained at a lower relative intensity than slower runners.[70] If running isn't for you, run slower. If it still isn't providing an instant reward, then walk. Get creative and try different variations of the same activity. If you don't find any immediate benefit in oil painting, try watercolours.

More learnings from Gestalt

Applying the Gestalt principle of proximity to our goals and ambitions unearthed several new opportunities for motivation scientists. If the proximity rule can be applied to merge actions and goals to help sustain hobbies, projects and lifestyle changes, can other Gestalt principles do the same?

Those clever Gestalt theorists also noticed that objects with shared visual characteristics are often perceived to be related, meaning that they are often stored in the brain as one larger composite object. When you see two people for the first time who look alike, you assume that they are related. Our brains take a leap and believe that anything with a similar design must be part of a larger entity. Companies use this mental process by using similar typographies and fonts. If you received a party invitation in the font of *Star Trek*, you'd link the party to the franchise and assume that there was an intergalactic theme to the shindig.

This mental approach is efficient, because storing one object in the brain is easier than two, but it can warp our perception of time and history, especially when we recall places and events outside of our personal experiences. The first time you heard or read that Cleopatra lived chronologic- ally closer in history to the building of the Shard in London (or any other contemporary building) than the construction of the Great Pyramid of Giza likely scrambled your mind a little. Unless you are a historian well versed in such details, your brain is likely to have lumped Cleopatra and Pyramid together under some umbrella term, such as 'ancient Egypt'. This union makes you think that Cleopatra was born in the same era as the Great Pyramid was built. However, it is esti- mated that Cleopatra was born in around 69 BCE, around 2,082 years before the Shard was opened. The Great Pyramid is thought to have been built in 2465 BCE, 2,396 years before Cleopatra's birth.

This effect is surprisingly common. Arguably the most famous of dinosaurs, largely thanks to the *Jurassic Park* film franchise, is the Tyrannosaurus rex. Ask a friend which spe- cies roamed the Earth nearer to the era of the T-rex: humans or the stegosaurus? Contrary to what you might expect, the

T-rex roamed the Earth in an era closer to the present day than the time that the stegosaurus lived. The stegosaurus was a herbivore found on planet Earth during the late Jurassic period, approximately 150 million years ago. It wasn't until over 80 million years later, around 68–66 million years ago, during the Cretaceous period, that the Tyrannosaurus rex roamed the Earth. Our brains fuse information about the Stegosaurus and the T-rex into a large collective term, likely to be 'dinosaurs'. This grouping makes us assume that they share other similarities, such as the period in which they lived.

Just like the proximity principle, the rule of similarity can be applied to reduce the gap between our actions and goals to enhance persistence in worthy activities. To achieve this, we can create semantically or linguistically similar actions and goals. When experimental participants were given the goal of improving performance on a computer game, their engagement was higher when the game was described as a game of 'skill' than when it was described as a game of 'fantasy'. This effect occurred because 'skill' is semantically like 'improve performance', whereas 'fantasy' is not.[71] Next time you are considering becoming healthier, don't go on a diet – just choose healthier foods. It's the same thing but with a different label. If you want to save money for a house deposit, make financial changes, rather than 'tightening your belt'. If you are looking to reduce stress, go for a relaxing run rather than doing some exercise. These seemingly insignificant changes to our language help the brain to reduce the motivational gap between our actions and the motivational power of our goals.

Gestalt scientists also discovered that if two separate objects act in the same way repeatedly, eventually they are likely to be perceived as the same entity. Several birds flying and changing direction synchronously are likely to be perceived as a flock, rather than individual birds. Once again, this idea can be applied to minimising the psychological gap between our actions and outcomes. If *reducing* food intake for a week leads to a corresponding *reduction* in weight, the action of dieting and the goal of losing weight are synchronous. Then, if the diet is stopped and the weight loss stops, they continue to be aligned. Eventually the connection between action and goal will get stronger and they will become fused. At work, if a sudden change in the timing of sales calls is successful in building the number of leads, then a link between the timing and success will be created. If further changes in timing also correspond to different levels of success, then a fused relationship will be established. In both scenarios, it will be easier to sustain the diet or the sales push because these actions have been merged with the motivational power of the outcome. Persistence is enhanced when actions and goals are synchronous. This principle might not provide a host of practical strategies that can enhance your mojo, but it does imply that you can benefit from adopting a scientific approach and monitoring your progress towards your personal goals. The only way you can identify which actions help you progress towards your goals most effectively is by measuring both action and progress to observe their relationship.

It is also possible to merge the motivation power of a goal that you value with one that you don't. Imagine two activities, one that you dislike and one that you like. Cooking dinner and listening to your favourite album might be an appropriate example. To encourage you to cook dinner, listen to the album at the same time. For decades, scientists have observed that pairing something relatively neutral (like cooking dinner) with something pleasant (like listening to your favourite album) establishes a relationship between them in the brain. Over time, the neutral event gets associated with the rewards of the positive event. Psychologists taught chimpanzees to insert tokens into a machine that automatically released a rewarding grape.[72] Once the chimps had begun to associate inserting tokens with the grape's pleasantness, they trained the chimps to lift a lever to get the tokens. The chimps began to value pulling the lever even though they no longer received a grape. The motivational power of grapes was transferred to lever pulls.

To take advantage of this principle, identify activities you do not enjoy, but are nonetheless important, and merge them with things that you do enjoy. If you're more of a client account manager than a sales hotshot but need to drum up some more business, then get yourself a favourite 'sales call' cake that you can munch through while making the calls (but no calls means no cake). If you only consume your favourite Black Forest gateau while trying to lure a new client, the motivational power of the cake will transfer to the sales calls. This trick is why most gym cardio equipment has integrated screens so you can watch your favourite Netflix drama while getting fit. However, this bundling of two activities will not have a motivational benefit if you also watch the drama at other times. Save *Bridgerton* for the treadmill.

Gestalt principles also tell us that a fusion will occur if two parts uniquely resemble each other more than any other parts. If you are at a crowded party and there is only one other person who dresses the same as you, then it's very likely that a bond will occur. Just like the other visual principles, we can apply this rule to reduce the gap between our actions and goals, and so enhance persistence. In one scientific experiment, participants were asked about the goal of keeping in shape and instructed to select one means of achieving this goal or three.[73] Participants who selected one method to keep in shape reported it as a more effective method than those who selected three methods. Similar effects were seen when the goal was to become popular. Unique relationships between actions and goals allow the motivational power of the goal to transfer more effectively to the action to help sustain it. Perhaps you want to be more sociable, and you decide to join a choir to achieve this goal. This represents a unique bond between activity and goal. However, if you decide to join a choir, go into the work office more and join a dating app, then the bond between joining a choir and being more sociable is not unique. Your motivation for the choir will not be as robust in the latter scenario, because the reward is diluted across three activities. In a similar way, associating the same activity with different outcomes also dilutes the relationship between action and goal. For any lifestyle changes or new projects that you want to commence, try to find a single, meaningful outcome and avoid focusing on several less impactful reasons for making these changes. For example, starting a new hobby should be done to be more creative *or* to meet new people *or* to learn a new skill. Focusing on all three will widen the gap between your actions and goals and reduce your motivation.

In a nutshell

German scientists and American advertising revolutionaries laid the foundations for establishing how to fuse different objects into one entity. Investigating how Gestalt visual principles can be applied to our actions and goals has led to significant leaps in what we know about human motivation. Optimum motivation is achieved when the means and the end, or the action and the outcome, are completely integrated. This state is critical for sustaining any new hobby, project or lifestyle change. Based on the vision and intellect of Gestalt scientists, we have several ways that we can fuse the means and the end to create robust motivation and greater persistence, and so get our mojos back. Reduce the time gap between activities and the rewards and outcomes that follow. Supplement this strategy by identifying goals and rewards that are semantically similar and creating unique bonds between a single action and single goal. Making these changes will take you back to your childhood, where motivation was at its purest and free from adult interference.

6

Happy endings

'If you want a happy ending, that depends, of course, on where you stop your story.'

– Orson Welles, movie-making
goliath and amateur magician

Tom Hanks has appeared in some of the biggest blockbusters of the last thirty years. He is only the second man to win the Best Actor Oscar in consecutive years, for his roles in *Philadelphia* and *Forrest Gump* (the first being Spencer Tracy in the 1930s, for *Captains Courageous* and *Boys Town*) – although many would argue that his best work was lending his voice to Woody the Cowboy in the *Toy Story* films.

What is less known about this Hollywood colossus is that, according to some of his celebrity friends, he regularly attends a party hosted by another movie legend, Steve Martin. These gatherings involve playing poker and watching movies, but also more unusual activities, such as avoiding solid foods, drinking liquids, taking laxatives and clearing their bowels. (Allegedly, the host only has one bathroom.) Martin and his guests' preparations are designed to make their otherwise daunting upcoming colonoscopy appointments a more comfortable experience, and hopefully make them less likely to avoid colonoscopies in the future. As it happens, this maligned surgical procedure has helped demonstrate how our feelings and memories are recalled differently according to their place in time. By focusing on the period prior to the colonoscopy, the movie legends are tackling the problem from the wrong angle. If you want to recall events more fondly, it's the end of the experience that is crucial. This process is a major factor in helping us decide whether to repeat or avoid activities in the future. Hanks, Martin and friends need a post-colonoscopy party in their social calendar.

When to finish the story

A colonoscopy is unlikely to be on many bucket lists. It involves a long, thin, flexible tube with a small camera inside it being passed into your anus to check inside your bowels. It would be sensible to assume that the longer the colonoscopy lasts, the more unpleasant the experience. However, speeding up this clinical invasion would be counterproductive, because it would not allow the influence of time to distort our recollection. When the colonoscope is left motionless inside for an extra three minutes after the procedure has finished, individuals typically report a more positive experience after the appointment compared to those who have the instrument removed immediately.[74] In other words, the recall of colonoscopies is often skewed by people's feelings at the climax, even if this means the experience lasts longer overall.

Scientists deliberately extended the colonoscopies of

patients because, some years earlier, a similar effect was unearthed when researchers asked university students to immerse a hand in iced water for a length of time.[75] Placing a hand in 15°C water is slightly less unpleasant than placing a hand in 14°C water, but both are unpleasant. The students overall reported a preference for a minute in 14°C water followed by thirty seconds of 15°C water, rather than just a minute of 14°C ice water. When asked which one they would repeat, more than two-thirds of the seemingly masochistic students selected the longer trial that meant greater overall discomfort. Most participants also reported that the longer trial was easier to cope with because it caused them *less* overall discomfort, and the coldest point was *less* cold than the shorter trial. The students held these false beliefs because humans don't typically judge events on the whole experience. We overemphasise the end.

Before healthcare specialists start extending the length of painful medical procedures, there's an ethical dilemma to be considered. Strictly speaking, patients will endure more discomfort than is strictly necessary if you extend the procedure. But which is more important, the length of discomfort a patient experiences in real time or the amount of discomfort a patient remembers? If asked, most patients will opt for a shorter procedure, even though that is likely to negatively influence future memories of the event. This debatable choice is due to an overly active desire for closure. In this context, closure does not mean coming to terms with a stressful event, like a relationship break-up. Motivational closure refers to the frequently illogical tendency to get tasks completed and goals achieved, even if this means a greater cost in the long term.[76]

In the colonoscopy example, most people will want the

experience over with and choose the quicker option, despite this choice leading to a more negative recalled experience. If you slowly and carefully peel a plaster off your skin with one hand while holding your skin taut with the other, it will not hurt. Yet most people adopt the 'rip it off quick' approach, despite some discomfort being likely. Some online car sales companies have built their entire business-marketing strategy on this bias. Many people prefer to sell their car easily to get the process over with quickly, even if it means getting less money for their car compared to other traditional methods. We want to get many things over with, even if it costs us in the long run. To paraphrase the quote from Orson Welles at the beginning of this chapter, people are often too eager to finish the story and miss the happier ending.

To describe this idea, the term 'pre-crastination' was coined in a series of scientific studies often labelled 'the bucket experiments'.[77] Before carrying out more complex tests, the research team needed to check that participants would prefer to carry the same load over a short distance, rather than a relatively longer distance. This seemingly pointless step was tested by placing two buckets at different distances in front of the participants and the finish line sixteen feet away from the start. They expected participants to choose the bucket that was further away because that one had to be carried a shorter distance overall. To the amazement of the researchers, participants tended to do the opposite. They were more likely to pick up the bucket closest to them, even though it was further away from the finish line.

The researchers conducted subsequent experiments to find out why this bizarre choice occurred. Participants did not carry the bucket further for exercise; the nearest bucket didn't grab their attention, nor did they believe that the bucket weights differed. The overwhelming reason was the belief that picking up the nearest bucket would get the task done sooner, even though the buckets were not heavy enough to alter walking speed so both options would take the same time to complete. The participants wanted to start ticking off steps in the pursuit of a larger goal. Thinking about a goal takes mental effort, so if there's a way to reduce this mental load, then people will often take up that option. Humans are not alone in possessing this bias. Pigeons also prefer to get a task started sooner rather than later, even though it makes no difference to the effort required or outcome obtained.[78] We have considerable difficulty allowing time to pass by inconspicuously when we have a task to accomplish.

In the same way, we often start the day on the little, unimportant jobs because of the urge to tick things off our to-do-list, even if it means more work in the long run. We waste time washing the few dishes after breakfast and then do the same again after lunch, when doing them once is quicker overall. Doing things too early means you can waste several hours on trivial tasks that didn't need doing. You know responding to an email will set off a cascade of tasks entering your in-tray, but you can't help it because you like an empty email inbox (the foolishness of this goal has already been discussed in chapter two). It seems we cannot allow time to flow without ruining it with trivial tasks. This quirk extends to paying more for services, such as hiring a plumber, if it means the task will be completed sooner. If you provide a service to the public, leverage this bias and charge more if they want the service sooner. For everyone else, make sure you're not

sacrificing the quality of an outcome simply for a quick solution. People (and pigeons) are motivated to start a task as soon
as possible so we can remove it from our mental load, often
in the false belief that this will lead to sooner completion or
less effort. While this might feel good at first, starting a goal
too early will often lead to time and effort wasted later. The
opposite side to this same flawed judgement often impedes
our progress on important tasks and projects that will take
a long time to achieve. Spending some time progressing on
these arduous-but-important tasks won't remove them from
our to-do-list, so we avoid doing so.

At times, the same principle can be applied to decision-
making. If a choice is weighing on your mind, it is tempting
to decide as soon as possible to remove the mental burden.
Instead, try letting the decision come to you over time, rather
than forcing it. Letting time pass and making decisions at
the last possible minute often allows you to incorporate the
maximum possible information, which means it's often easier
to decide quickly. Sometimes if you wait long enough, the
decision becomes irrelevant, so you no longer need to make it
at all. Don't try to fill your time with needless thinking and
rush major decisions, even if it is tempting to do so.

Rigging the vote

The colonoscopy and iced-water experiments demonstrated
that participants were skewed towards remembering the end
phases of these events, rather than the whole episode. But not
many of us have colonoscopies, and even fewer routinely stick
our hands in iced water. Nonetheless, this overemphasis on

the final phase of events influences our lives in many other ways, and sometimes not for the best.

A US presidential term typically lasts for four years, and UK general elections usually take place every four or five years. When it is time to vote, any government knows that their economic performance tends to be a crucial factor considered by voters. The former UK prime minister Harold Wilson stated that 'the standing of the government and its ability to hold the confidence of the electorate at the general election depend on the success of its economic policy'. A reminder placed in the office of ex-president Bill Clinton during the 1992 election read: 'It's the economy, stupid.' It might be assumed that the governing party's economic performance over the whole term is central to voters' decisions. Indeed, when voters are asked how they will decide who to vote for, this is exactly what they suggest they will consider.

But this is not what happens, despite voters' logical intentions. The state of the economy during the lead-up to the election influences voting much more than economic performance over the entire term of the governing party.[79] In other words, it's the governing party's economic performance *at the end of their term* that is important. This bias is partly why there was some surprise at then-UK prime minister Rishi Sunak's decision to call for a general election in May 2024, just as the UK's stalling economy was predicted to improve. Despite the intention to consider economic performance over the entire term, this information is difficult to acquire for voters. This difficulty can be literal because the information is not conveyed in the news, which emphasises *current* affairs, so often only economic aficionados have the wherewithal and desire to search for relevant figures online. Even if the information is readily available, it can still be too effortful for the brain to evaluate the whole event. As a result, voters go for the next best thing: *recent* economic performance, which is readily available in the news and can be used as a proxy for *overall* economic performance. Financial analysis of the 2000 US election showed that, had voters considered the whole term instead of the final months, they would have elected Al Gore instead of George W. Bush.[80] Our unequal recall of events depending on their place in time shapes the global political landscape. As Nobel Prize-winning psychologist Daniel Kahneman wrote: 'When faced with a difficult question, we often answer an easier one instead, usually without noticing the substitution.'

Our brains retrieve memories of experiences in the same way. When we recall an experience, the human brain simplifies things and assumes the later moments are a good proxy for the whole episode. This effect is somewhat different from our recall of *lists* of objects, facts or information. In this case, the first and last items are typically remembered most vividly. If you were asked to remember a dog, cow, sheep, rabbit and cat, it is the canine and feline that would be recalled with most ease. This memorisation is due to the primacy effect (you remember the first object) and the recency effect (you remember the last object). In contrast, when we are recalling *experiences*, it is our feelings in the final phases that are most influential. These contrasting effects occur because the two types of recall require different brain activity. Remembering lists requires short-term memory and attention function, whereas evaluating how we felt about an event occurs rapidly and at low levels of consciousness. It is designed as an impulsive, simple and efficient response that does not require significant mental processing. At amusement parks, people remember the ride, not the queue (unless the queue is so long that it creates particularly intense feelings – more on this later).

These two different functions have implications for things like jury decisions. One might expect that evidence presented at the beginning of the trial is more influential in the jury's decision because they are likely to be fresh and alert. On the other hand, the evidence at the end is the most recent, so freshest in the memory. Both possibilities are likely if the jurors assess the plausibility of guilt factually. However, if the defendant's case is based on emotional content and the lawyers want the jury to side with their client, then the final phases of the trial strongly influence the verdict. Likewise, you will also retrospectively assess an advert based largely on the final moments of the clip.

In the run-up to the 2012 election, Barack Obama tried to override voters' reliance on the end phases to emphasise his Democratic Party's performance across the whole term, which was pretty good. With the assistance of the US media's emphasis on the current economy, voters had other ideas and stressed recent economic performance, which wasn't as strong. Obama still won, but with thirty-three fewer seats than he won in 2008. As a side issue, the power of the media should not be underestimated in such matters. In the run-up to the 1997 UK election, the governing Conservative party performed well economically, but the media coverage did not tell the same story. Analysis of the major TV evening news programmes suggested that the coverage was not as positive as it should have been to reflect true performance. For example, the coverage often focused on major party splits on economic policy, rather than the actual policies that were implemented successfully. The Conservatives went on to record one of their worst election results in history.[81]

An underhand way that politicians leverage our tendency to remember recent events is to actively focus on growing the economy or launching popular policies in the last year before an election, not the whole term. This creates a bias towards flagship, safe-bet policies occurring in the final stretch of a term. Implementing these policies earlier would lead them to be ignored when the public is choosing who to vote for some years later. On the flip side, there's also a tendency to implement less popular policies early on in their term because they are more likely to be forgotten. This election-year focus can lead voters to choose the best manipulator who saves their big policies for the end, rather than the best leader.

Intense moments are memorable moments

Our voting behaviour is one example of our brain's distaste for evaluating a whole experience: it's too mentally taxing to obtain all the information, so we recall the end parts of the experience in the often false belief that they reflect the whole episode. This temporal bias can be magnified according to how accessible information is in the brain. People wrongly inflate the probability of an airplane crash if they have recently read about an airplane crash because the information is readily accessible. This bias can represent a problem when events like injuries during exercise occur. If you strain a muscle when going for a jog, you will falsely inflate the probability that you will get injured again if you go for a jog, because the information is accessible. This false belief will reduce the likelihood of you continuing with your jogging plans. If you experience a setback in any context, you are similarly likely to overinflate the probability of it occurring again.

This bias towards accessible information first came to prominence in the 1970s in an experiment by the previously mentioned Daniel Kahneman and his fellow pioneer of psychology and economics, Amos Tversky. Participants were asked whether more words begin with the letter K (e.g., king) or contain the letter K (e.g., cake). Most people will plump for words beginning with the letter K, and they'd be like the seventy per cent of participants in the experiment who did the same. However, they'd be wrong. There are many more words containing K than beginning with K.[82] The problem is that words beginning with K are more easily available in the brain, so these are emphasised when making a quick calculation.

Accessibility and recall are enhanced by the intensity of feeling that an event provokes.[83] Major geopolitical events tend to be very emotive and accessible to the brain when we evaluate the past. The Covid-19 pandemic and the September 11 terrorist attacks were mega-events that significantly disrupted much of the world and have left indelible marks on our lives. Politicians and their people behind the scenes use this quirk of memory to make some policies memorable. For example, completing Brexit and reducing immigration were pledges that were likely to be popular among large demographics. Hence, the Conservative party attached the emotive slogans 'Get Brexit done' and 'Stop the boats' to them, which makes it easier for people to remember them in the lead-up to elections. There are no such slogans attached to the raising of taxes or reducing public funding. We remember these massive events and government policies well, not because they occurred at the end of an experience, but because of the intense feelings that they trigger. In the same way, a mundane party is remembered fondly because of the five minutes spent flirting with the attractive fellow guest. A great dinner, though, will be recalled negatively if the waiter spills wine on your favourite outfit. Intense moments are memorable moments.

Starbucks shows it is the master of the memorable experience by having customers' names written on their cups. Someone asking your name creates a positive feeling and creates opportunity for conversation in an otherwise mundane and forgetful interaction. Starbucks also developed their pay-it-forward chains, designed so some customers unexpectedly get their coffee for free (although this concept was not universally liked, especially by the baristas). These are all small ways that Starbucks makes you keep coming back, by creating positive feelings and providing a memorable experience.

A visit to the dentist is a common example of how intense negative moments distort our memories and subsequent evaluations. Few people look forward to seeing the dentist, primarily because it is perceived as a wholly unpleasant experience. Yet almost all dentist appointments pass without major incident. Our perceptions become skewed by the rare moment when the dentist catches a sensitive part of a tooth and you need to be peeled off the ceiling. Then the whole appointment is likely to be stored as a negative experience. This memory is very likely to put someone off from visiting again because of the desire to avoid repeat pain. But, counterintuitively, avoiding the dentist makes pain in the future more likely. Our biased evaluations of the past impact our future choices, including those that have significant consequences for our health and wellbeing.

Creating intense moments so that the information is readily accessible in the brain is arguably the cornerstone principle of the advertising industry. Adverts are intended to make you *feel* something about the brand, so that when you need to shop for that type of product, the memory is accessible, and you purchase that brand. Lottery adverts are designed to create an emotional reaction to falsely enhance your calculations on how likely you are to win the lottery. This effect is also why emotionally charged news headlines about a terrorist attack by someone of a specific ethnicity are so dangerous. The emotional intensity creates memories that stick in our minds, and we overinflate the chances of another terrorist attack from someone of the same ethnicity.

By controlling the timing of the most intense parts of an event to coincide with the end phases of our experiences, we can substantially amplify our recall. Manufacturing our lives in this way will have significant implications for sustaining new activities or lifestyle changes. The most intense experience and the climax are the easiest to access for our brains, so we should always try to end on the highest note if we want to repeat that activity. Nature is excellent at adhering to this principle to encourage procreation. The male orgasm is an example of a motivating final experience that encourages us to repeat the act. The exhilarating end of successful childbirth outweighs the overall painful and exhausting experience when impulsively recalling the event. On the other hand, intense but negative final moments can have equally lasting effects. In an experiment, sixty-four women watched a clip from the horror film *The Strangers*.[84] Half of the women finished the clip at the most frightening moment (as determined by the heart rate of previously tested participants). The other half watched the same clip but extended to include a slightly less frightening ending. The women who ended with the most frightening scene reported more anxiety after the clip had ended. When summarising over 170 studies that examined our recall of different experiences, researchers found convincing evidence that we rely heavily on the most intense and final moments of the event.[85] When these two effects are combined, our recollection becomes even more biased.

The influence on our recall of the most intense moments and the climax varies. The impact of the most intense moments tends to fade over time. In contrast, the climax increases its impact on our recall as time passes by. The more the experience drifts into history, the more our brains rely on the end phases as an indicator of the whole event. When someone asks you about a holiday a couple of weeks ago, your brain will emphasise the end period to some degree, but it's still relatively easy to access other aspects. However, when someone asks you about a holiday several years ago, it's too laborious for your brain to evaluate the whole holiday, so it focuses largely on the end. The final phase of experience becomes even more important for our evaluations as time passes.

These biases and how we evaluate past events are key to our future engagement in similar events. When we begin to decide whether to exercise, work, cook a nice meal, paint a picture, read a book or do any other activity, we unconsciously and quickly access these past evaluations to help us decide whether to do it or remain reclined on the sofa. These evaluations often hide themselves behind other overt reasons not to do an activity. For example, our rapid evaluation of a cooking class might be somewhat negative, so when we decide whether to go to the class next week, this initial appraisal leads us to reflect on a perceived lack of time and we don't go. In this example, it is the recall of the previous experience that is the true cause of not attending, not the lack of time.

Putting theory into practice

Beyond voting, water torture and colonoscopies, we can apply these mental processes to improve our everyday lives. In an experiment, scientists designed two different weight-training sessions that were identical in intensity.[86] One was increasingly uncomfortable because it got progressively harder, while the other was progressively easier, so the end was relatively comfortable. During the sessions, participants rated their experience of the sessions equally positively. However, when they were asked to rate their experience at the end, and again some time after the session, participants remembered the progressively easier session more fondly. If you are new to exercise and want to sustain your exercise regime, complete the difficult exercises early and make the end a more positive experience. This tip can be applied to any other hobby or project you wish to undertake. If you want to go back to something again and again, make the end the most pleasurable aspect.

This principle doesn't have to be employed to enhance the likelihood of sustaining an activity; it can simply be used to make you remember things more fondly. A holiday will be evaluated as having been better if a five-hour delay to your flight occurs at the beginning, rather than the end. This idea can be adapted by making the return trip, or at least the final elements of the journey, as easy as possible when planning a holiday. When booking holiday travel, if you have a choice between a lengthy, awkward outward leg and a straight- forward return leg, or vice versa, take the former option. Choosing to finish with the easier leg will provide warmer recollections of the overall holiday.

These rules can also be applied to educational settings, or to providing feedback in general. Following an assessment, scientists provided children with either four negative ratings from peers, or four negative ratings plus a slightly less nega- tive rating.[87] In a similar way to the colonoscopy, children who received more overall negative feedback illogically remembered the assessment as more positive and less difficult to cope with. The experimenters also flipped the idea and gave some students four positive ratings, and others four positive ratings and a fifth slightly less positive rating. This final fifth rating led to the children reporting the assessment as less posi- tive and more difficult to cope with, even though they received more positive feedback overall. Teachers and parents, beware of your final statements to children, because they can leave very different tastes in the mouth.

The way we recollect over time means that a happy ending is better than a shorter task. For activities in which the most intense moment is unpleasurable, the same strategy applies, but in reverse. It's prudent to try to make sure the unpleasant moments occur at the beginning of the event. If you are dread- ing giving your essential work presentation in the monthly meeting, volunteer to present first. If there's a difficult con- versation to be had at the family gathering, don't beat around the bush if you want to remember the occasion more fondly.

When you are a customer receiving a service, take note of these biases. Customer experiences that have notable positive peaks, such as a surprise discount or competition, are likely to be remembered more positively, even though the overall experience might not have been any better than others. Everyone remembers the singing ticket inspector on the train, even if there's a delay to the journey. I remember the unexpected glass of fizz while checking in at a hotel in Seville, and little else about the venue. Equally, don't let a somewhat negative end to an experience blur what was an otherwise pleasant experience. I often get overly disappointed at restaurants when the bill takes a while to arrive, even though the rest of the service has been exemplary.

If your work involves customer service, take advantage of these biases. If possible, the positive experience should be engineered to occur at the end. The shop assistant or security guard by the exit has a critical role to play in customer experience. A grumpy assistant can substantially damage the recollection of the whole shop experience. On the other hand, a surprisingly funny conversation can override any issues queuing at the checkout. Customers will implicitly recall the product or service fondly, and be more likely to return and purchase more goods. Sometimes a negative aspect of the customer experience is inevitable. Telling a customer, for example, that their product has been damaged during transit is not going to go down well. Make sure negative moments like these happen in the early phases of the interaction and, most importantly, deal with it well. If the last interactions with a customer involve you dealing with a problem satisfactorily, it can turn a negative experience into a positive one.

These human biases towards the end periods and the most intense moments also have implications for the pricing of products. When we evaluate different products, the brain will typically form a reference price that offers a comparison to all other prices. Economists have investigated how individuals form these reference prices.[88] It turns out that the reference price is largely based on the last price viewed and the peak price of the different products. In other words, we follow the same rules when we evaluate product prices as we do when we recall events. If a company sporadically raises the price of the highest-priced product, our reference price is also raised, which means we will tolerate higher prices. On the flip side, luxury brands will rarely offer big discounts because this will significantly lower our reference price and reduce the amount we will pay for the product in the future. The take-home message is to be conscious of these types of price manipulation. The most expensive bottle of wine might be on the menu simply to increase the amount that you are willing to pay for other bottles on the list. If the last car model that you are shown is the most expensive, it might be because the salesperson wants to raise your reference price and make you part with more money than you were originally willing to. Rolls-Royce adopt these tactics by displaying their cars at air shows. If the last thing you viewed was a private jet retailing at several million pounds, then your reference price will be astronomical, and a £250,000 Rolls-Royce will look like a bargain.

How the order and intensity of our experiences impacts on our recall and wellbeing has also been applied to the staff turnover of volunteer-crisis counsellors. Nearly two million phone calls were examined to establish whether volunteers were more or less likely to quit their roles depending on the occurrence of difficult suicide-prevention conversations (as opposed to conversations not related to suicide).[89] Trying to

stop somebody from ending their life is likely to be emotionally very intense and taxing, so it's unsurprising that the more
suicide-related conversations a volunteer was involved in,
the more likely they were to stop volunteering. Less obvious
was the idea that the *order* of past interactions also counted.
Just like the recall of events, suicide-prevention conversations at the end of a sequence of phone calls led to a stronger
likelihood of volunteers quitting their roles. Suicide-related
conversations also increased the probability of volunteers
quitting if they occurred in streaks. Over a session, three
suicide-prevention calls in a row at the end of the shift would
lead to greater probability of quitting the volunteer role, compared to three suicide-prevention calls spaced out over the
shift, or if they occurred earlier.

These trends have major implications for healthcare.
Having emotionally intense and demanding appointments
with patients is inevitable for many healthcare professionals,
but they can be reordered so that streaks of these challenging
appointments are avoided, and the appointments themselves
are completed earlier in the day. Manufacturing schedules
in this way will lead to less burnout and quitting in healthcare professions, which means more lives are saved. The
researchers involved in the crisis-volunteer study mathemat-
ically modelled what would happen if this reordering took
place, and they estimated a twenty-two per cent reduction
in quitting.

Of course, there are some circumstances when it is necessary to prevent these biases swaying recollections and
there's a need for objectivity. You don't want to recruit a job
candidate just because they were last to be interviewed and
cracked a funny joke. Do you really want to return to that

holiday destination, or was it just the final day that was good? Totally removing these biases is impossible because they are a well-functioning brain process developed over hundreds of generations. A good way to account for them is to mimic cyber security. 'Red teams' are a group of individuals who pretend to be the enemy and aim to hack into a company's cyber network. They help identify faults in the network that could be a weakness ripe for hacking. In your own work context, such as job interviews, you can nominate individuals who deliberately go against group thinking to check for biases in decision-making. In your personal life, you can nominate a friend or relative to be your critical sounding board when making big life decisions, like moving house or changing job. Another option requiring some self-awareness is to put on your own red hat and actively take different perspectives that conflict with your natural thinking, seeking out these biases before making big decisions.

Create intensity through novelty

Unfortunately, some incidents are completely beyond our control. We cannot account for a delayed train home ruining our experience of an otherwise fine visit to the seaside, or losing a phone on a fun night out. But we can stack the odds in our favour. A *novel* experience at the end of an activity is pure opium for your mojo and motivation.[90] The telecommunications industry often gets a bad rap for customer experience. We've all spent twenty minutes on hold before someone at the other end explains they are unable to help with our Wi-Fi problem. However, AT & T gave two thousand of their customers a memorable experience at the end of an interaction by sending novel personalised thank-you videos for their custom. This small but significant tactic will create a more favourable memory.

Novelty creates more intense feelings compared to normality because it is important to add these unique experiences to our memories. Like most adaptive brain processes, this developed in our evolutionary past. Exploring novel surroundings or situations helped our ancestors gain new knowledge important for survival, such as where to find food and essential resources. Because novelty became associated with enhanced survival, our ancestors' brains encouraged novelty-seeking by releasing dopamine into their bodies.[91] As we know from chapter three, dopamine is biology's way of making us feel good as a reward and to encourage us to do it again. This dopamine release is experienced as a positive emotion. Novelty creates emotionally intense moments.

If we continually experience the same stimuli, called habituation, then our brains start to ignore unimportant aspects to save brain power.[92] If something is familiar, then it's unlikely we will learn anything new if we focus on it. For example, when you walk into a room and smell something for the first time, the smell will be quite potent and will create an emotional reaction, so you remember it. If you then walk into that room every day, you will gradually become accustomed to that smell. The smell doesn't go away; it just provokes less of a response each time you encounter it. This habituation is associated with lower dopamine and less emotional responses each time you encounter the stimulus.

To further aid novel experiences embedding themselves in our memories, the length of novel events is also overestimated compared to typical experiences. When novel images are occasionally and randomly shown among repeated images to experimental participants, the novel images seem to appear for longer than the repeated images, even though the timings are equal.[93] I recently fell off my bike because I was too busy gazing at farm animals to notice an unusually large bump in the road. Because hurtling towards tarmac is a novel experience, it seemed like time passed in slow motion. Likewise, victims of car accidents often report that the crash seemed longer than it was, partly because it was novel and surrounded by mundane events. Childhood is full of novelty, so time passes more slowly compared to adulthood. Novelty is memorable because it is seemingly extended and emotionally intense.

Inserting novelty at the end of an activity can have profound effects for those needing to sustain such activities in the long term. Business owners, give your customers a novel gesture on departure and they are more likely to return. Who doesn't like a free taster as they leave the food shop? But don't overdo it, or the novelty wears off. Parents, try to provide some novelty at the end of a mundane activity, like your child cleaning their bedroom or eating their greens, if you want them to repeat it. Maybe putting on a catchy new song might just get your little angels to tidy up the mass destruction they have created in the lounge. Gym-goers, try something new at the end of the session to sustain healthy routines and motivation. Maybe try that weird-looking machine in the corner of the weights room or learn a different exercise. If you have started walking to get healthier, try to vary the route a little or even look up at the higher floors of buildings you pass by for a novel perspective. It's amazing what different things you'll observe.

Novelty can be scary. Your standard Silicon Valley

entrepreneur doesn't baulk at the idea of novelty, but a lot of people hesitate when the opportunity to do something new presents itself. But novelty doesn't have to mean taking excessive risks. Clinical psychologists have long known that excessive novelty-seeking can be associated with unnecessarily risky behaviour and sometimes leads to mental illness. Novelty in a motivational context means looking for different ways of thinking, taking a different approach to a task, and so on. Walking a different path to your favourite coffee shop or changing your running route will make a small positive difference to your outlook and motivation.

Often, a novel experience can be achieved simply by being more mindful of your surroundings. Many scientific theories suggest that an openness to novelty is a central feature of being mindful.[94] Familiar environments suddenly become novel when you focus on something different. Our most used sense is sight, for example, but if we change to focus on what we hear, smell or feel, then new aspects of familiar situations materialise. These little and simple life changes will give you a small injection of positive emotion and help you recall events positively. Sometimes novelty is confused with complexity, but simplifying an experience can be novel too. If you are learning something new, for example, a look at the simpler aspects can be a refreshing departure from trying to learn the most difficult components.

In a nutshell

When we are trying to decide whether to do an activity again, like taking a language lesson or exercise class, or revisiting a shop, our brains consider past similar experiences. This is done at a very low level of consciousness, because it needs to be done quickly and efficiently. As a result, our brains do not evaluate the whole experience, but instead focus on the end period and when feelings were most intense. The end is the brain's most frequently accessed section of time. To help us sustain meaningful but effortful activities, we can exercise this quirk by making sure our experiences are shaped in specific ways. Put the most enjoyable aspect at the end of a gruelling exercise session, and you are more likely to remember it fondly. Give customers a pleasant, unexpected send-off and they are more likely to return. Using novelty to create intense emotional responses will help us look back at events more warmly and can make sustaining our lifestyle changes or new projects more likely.

7

'S' is for effort

'Endure and persist; this pain will turn to good by and by.'

– Ovid, Roman poet

Laozi, the founder of Taoism, is said to be the originator of a Chinese proverb that has developed into this modern phrase:

'A journey of a thousand miles begins with a single step.'

This phrase encourages people to initiate a significant project by focusing on the first task and ignoring the bigger picture. You may want to own a fashion empire to rival Chanel, but this is likely to remain a pipe dream unless you focus on researching your competition and potential market. If you aim to control the world, do not focus on global domination; focus on one country at a time. As well as its catchiness, Laozi's advice is remarkable in its overlap with basic physical principles. A state of inertia means that any physical object will continue in its existing motionless state unless extra force is applied to it. The more mass the object possesses, the greater the inertia, and the more physical force is required for motion. Once the object is moving, inertia reduces and much less force is required to keep it moving. Just like Laozi's suggestion, focusing on the first task to overcome inertia will literally get the ball rolling.

We can combine this philosophical and physical insight to explain 'motivational inertia'. Human effort follows the same principle as physical objects. We need relatively large amounts of effort to start any task, but once it has commenced, it takes much less effort to sustain motion or progress. Once you've stepped out of the door, a jog is much easier to sustain. Once the fresh ingredients have been taken out of the fridge, a home-cooked meal is more likely to end up on the plate. Once you've made the first sales call, energy is on your side. Understanding motivational inertia helps to clarify that a major obstacle to a new hobby, project or lifestyle choice is starting it. Humans have incredible difficulty employing sufficient effort to initiate an activity.

Unfortunately, the high levels of effort required to overcome motivational inertia and begin a new project are compounded by our general aversion to effort.[95] Prehistoric survival was too precarious to go wasting energy on a nice walk up a hill to admire the view. Energy was required to fight off infection and illness, to hunt for food and to escape predators. Energy reserves were also needed in case food stocks ran dry. Energy conservation was so essential to survival that the human brain evolved to bias decision-making towards minimising effort. When deciding between different actions, humans are inclined to select the least effortful option. This prejudice applies to physical effort, such as running or walking, and mental effort, such as making a difficult decision or putting it off for later. For our predecessors, if a decision had to be made between going hunting or staying put next to the fire, then it's likely the latter option would be chosen except in drastic circumstances.

The start of the twentieth century saw living conditions rapidly improve. As we have seen in earlier chapters, the speed of environmental and technological development over the last two centuries has meant that many of our adaptations have become dysfunctional in our contemporary surroundings. Similarly, the life-prolonging advantages of avoiding effort have vanished thanks to the environment we have created. It is no longer worth saving effort just in case we get infected or stumble across an animal looking to eat us. In fact, humans have created a situation in which *using* effort rather than *saving* it should be prioritised. As a species, we consume more nutritional energy than ever, yet numerous technological advances have made life less effortful. Many of us do not leave our homes to go to work – or, if we do, we drive a car to get there. We only leave our desk to go to the bathroom (when will this inconvenience be removed?). At home, delivery companies can bring our food, and an algorithm recommends the evening entertainment. A few quick swipes on a dating app, and we have identified a partner for the evening. Life-or-death emergencies are scarce. If a choice existed between walking to get your Crispy Szechuan Beef Chinese takeaway meal or getting it delivered for free, the shoes stay in the cupboard for most people, most of the time. Our brains are designed to *save* effort, yet we think it can help us *use* effort. It is foolish to expect our brains to help us visit the gym when they think that sitting on the sofa will enhance our chances of survival.

From a motivational perspective, effort is a major barrier, and we need to sidestep our natural inclinations.

Often, this prehistoric tendency biased our decisions towards maintaining the status quo, because this was often the easier and less risky option. For example, it was much less effort to continue to exploit current food reserves than it was to go and hunt for new supplies. It was risky to spend limited energy when it might be required in a life-or-death emergency later. If something wasn't broken, then we didn't try to fix it. This motivational quirk is a major reason why our ambitions and goals remain unfulfilled. As ex-US president Theodore Roosevelt noted: 'Nothing in the world is worth having unless it means effort.' Most things worth pursuing, like setting up a new business, getting fit or writing a book, require significant amounts of effort. Yet our brains paradoxically tell us to avoid effort whenever possible. Many goals or objectives are daunting. Training for a marathon or developing a successful new business, for example, are mammoth undertakings that require indeterminable levels of effort. It's unsurprising that our tendency to avoid effort is triggered and combines with motivational inertia to keep our ambitions unrealised.

Overcoming inertia

Motivational inertia and our tendency to avoid effort should not prevent us from setting grand goals. Ambitious and difficult goals can excite us, reduce boredom and prevent stagnation. Our capacity for learning, curiosity and exploration is driven by ambition and the lofty goals that we set. We should set massive goals, but they are not sufficient to motivate us on a daily basis. Aiming for difficult goals excites, but it doesn't consistently motivate us to act, at least in the early stages of a project when we are trying to overcome inertia.

The first action to take in order to overcome motivational inertia seems straightforward but is often incorrectly implemented. As Laozi advised, focus on the first step, not the thousand-mile journey. When starting a new activity, hobby, challenge or project, we need to stack the odds in our favour by making the effort required as little as possible. This means breaking down larger, more ambitious goals into incredibly small short-term goals. Breaking down the overall project or activity into a tiny first chunk or sub-task will lower the effort required to overcome inertia. The emphasis here should be placed on *incredibly* small and tiny. For example, the thought of starting a work project, educational course or fitness programme might be intimidating because it seems such a daunting task. The mistake often made is that the sub-task is not small enough, and individuals still try to take big leaps to conquer the thousand miles, rather than single steps. Thanks to inertia pushing against you, the effort required to start a project is significantly inflated, so the sub-task needs to be *tiny* to counteract this inflation. The smaller the goal, the smaller the inertia to overcome.

For example, an individual new to fitness may start a running programme with the long-term goal of being able to run five kilometres. They may break this target down and focus on running one kilometre, but for many people that still requires a large amount of effort that is inflated by inertia, so the target remains too daunting. A more effective target would be to put on running shoes and step out the door. This goal is small enough that the added effort required to overcome inertia is more likely to be overcome. Scientific evidence suggests that patients with more modest weight-loss goals make greater progress than those with ambitious goals.[96] If you are developing a successful business, the first sub-target might be to develop a business plan, but a superior one would be to download a business-plan template. If you have never saved money before, try to save one pound, not one hundred. If you want to write a book, aim to write a sentence, not a page.

If initiating the first task remains a struggle, break it down into increasingly smaller chunks until you can overcome motivational inertia. If this strategy is still not working, don't forget all the seemingly insignificant preparation that needs to be done before you can start any task. For example, if you want to start going for a walk every morning, your goal should be to place your shoes in a convenient spot by the door. If you are writing a book and writing a sentence is too daunting, then aim to open your laptop. These preparatory tasks are still tasks and goals that need to be achieved. It's much easier to overcome inertia when the little barriers have been removed and you've greased the wheels. Including preparatory tasks in your planning will help start big projects and life-enhancing activities. It doesn't matter if the first step is apparently trivial, because the aim is to get started.

As well as helping you to overcome inertia, setting micro goals will (almost) guarantee success, which is psychologically rewarding (who doesn't like experiencing success?) and also has lesser-known biological consequences. Achieving goals works in a similar way to cocaine – albeit at a significantly lower intensity – by stimulating dopamine and serotonin in the brain, both of which create rewarding feelings of satisfaction and happiness. These feelings motivate us to seek the same experience again. Fortunately, by setting small goals we get hooked on success, rather than a class-A drug.

Success has other remarkable cerebral consequences. The brain continually goes through a process called neuroplasticity, which means it is continually developing or degrading over time. As scientific methods advance, we have begun to understand the causes of these changes – in monkeys, at least. When monkeys were rewarded with some tasty fruit juice for successfully accomplishing a task, neural networks in their brains were activated for several seconds. When the monkeys failed the task, there was no weakening of networks.[97] These findings imply that success changes the neurological structure of your brain and helps you learn. What's more, failure only has adverse effects on your brain when it has meaningful consequences. This means that setting and reaching for small goals is a no-lose scenario for your brain development.

Once you have reduced the effort required to achieve tasks, the second strategy is to remove any unnecessary effort in your planned activity. In 1948, military physician Thomas DeLorme wrote in the scientific press that performing an exercise for three sets of ten repetitions was optimal for physical strength benefits.[98] A few years later, an English surgeon named Ian McQueen, who happened to be a competitive bodybuilder, recommended a similar number of sets and repetitions for optimal muscle growth.[99] Over seventy years later, there remains a dogmatic allegiance to this belief that resistance-training exercises must be done for three sets, each comprising eight to twelve repetitions. Fitness experts in the 1950s also recommended that runners should not drink any fluid during a marathon race, and that vibrating belt machines should be used to shake fat from the body. Like many other false exercise beliefs from the 1950s, three sets for resistance training should be resigned to the history books.

Arthur Jones was a pioneer in the exercise field in the seventies and eighties. He teamed up with researchers from Colorado State University to conduct an experiment that discovered doing one set until you can no longer do another repetition improved strength and endurance far beyond doing the conventional three sets.[100] Using bigger weights makes muscle fibres grow larger, whereas increasing repetitions improves the muscles' ability to process and use energy. But if you simply slow your exercise movement down, you achieve both benefits and make the same gains in one set as you would do in three sets. In other words, Jones was recommending a 'minimum effective dose', which is a term used in clinical settings to describe the lowest amount of an intervention (usually a drug) required to provide a meaningful response. The minimum effective dose is much lower than most people think. Despite this effect being demonstrated over fifty years ago, it is still not well accepted in the mainstream.

Establishing the minimum effective dose can be done for all our tasks, projects and ambitions, not just getting fitter and stronger. Look for any unnecessary effort in your plans to identify the *minimum effective effort*. The executive summary at the beginning of a report is not just for executives. Almost everyone only needs to read this section, not the one-hundred-page report. It takes much less effort to eat healthily than most people think. How much do you really need to save for that holiday? Do you really need all those people to attend that project meeting? Can you cut out the middleman in some work projects? Unnecessary effort is everywhere if you look for it.

Once the initial motivational inertia has been overcome, you are in an advantageous position. Isaac Newton's second law of motion explains that force = mass × acceleration. An implication of this rule is that, once inertia has been overcome, much less force is required to keep an object moving, or even to get it to move faster. Conversely, an object that is moving fast requires more force to stop it than an object with the same mass that is moving slowly. This idea describes momentum, and we can apply this principle to our goals and dreams. If you overcome inertia and make small progress in a new hobby or towards a new goal, you will start developing momentum. Similarly, once your day has started productively and you have gained momentum, it requires much less effort to keep it progressing (which is another reason why starting activities as soon as possible was recommended in chapter three). Nonetheless, it's not all plain sailing from here. Our motivation and effort over the course of a task waxes and wanes, providing us with weak points and opportunities.

'S' is for effort

I'm fortunate to work somewhere that has been voted the world's number-one place to study sport for several years running. This provides me with regular opportunities to observe and learn about high-quality athletes' training. The physiological tests that many athletes go through can be brutal, with vomiting or collapsing at the end of the test being common. Nonetheless, watching these physical specimens reveals a great deal about the relationship between time and effort. When athletes perform a simulated time trial on a stationary bike in a laboratory, the power that they exert can be continuously monitored. This power, measured in watts, is a measure of their physical effort over the course of the trial. Tests like these reveal that the physical effort exerted follows an extremely predictable trend. Effort will quickly increase at the beginning of the task, often to a level that would be unsustainable over the whole trial. This spike in effort reflects the athlete overcoming inertia and producing more force to start pedalling than is required to keep pedalling.

During the next phase of the test, effort is guaranteed to decline. The athlete will recalibrate their efforts once inertia has been overcome, which then causes a reduction in effort. The brain also likes the body to be in a restful state, called homeostasis, because there is very little risk of malfunction. Any significant deviations from homeostasis cause the brain to encourage a reduction of effort to bring the body back to a restful state. The brain also leans towards conservatism when deciding whether the current effort can be maintained throughout the trial, which further encourages a reduction in effort.

During the final phases of the time trial, athletes will reliably increase their efforts. The conservatism shown in the middle section is overridden because it becomes easier to establish what levels of effort can be sustained over shorter periods. People typically work harder when they are near the finish line, because the goal is within reach, achievable and more motivating. This upturn in effort is unusually but routinely observed in a popular TV show called *Race Across the World*. Teams of two, usually a parent and child, siblings, a couple or a pair of friends, must race from one point in the world to another with several checkpoints in between. For example, in the first series, participants raced from London to Singapore. Participants are given money equivalent to a one-way plane ticket but cannot travel by air. They are not permitted mobile electronic devices or credit cards, and start with just a world map and a travel guide. Each stage of the race is several hundred kilometres long, such as from London to Greece. Despite these stages taking several days, it is remarkable how often the teams get to within a few hundred metres of the checkpoint and then start running. The time taken by the pairs is measured in days, rather than seconds, yet even the oldest, most impaired participants break into a jog for seemingly futile reasons. The human tendency to raise effort at the end of a task is pervasive.

Scientists call this complete pattern of effort over time a cubic function, but for non-scientists it is often called an 'S curve' (albeit a horizontal, flattened-out S curve).[101] This pattern is so reliable that even when athletes are asked to maintain a consistent effort over a period, they are unable to do so. This S curve is even more pronounced in people who aren't athletes, because they do not possess as much prior experience of exhausting themselves and cannot monitor their efforts accordingly.

It is not only physical effort that follows an S curve; the use of mental effort follows an identical pattern. The beginning and end of a task or project are the points at which people tend to work hardest and are most conscientious. High mental effort is required to overcome inertia at the beginning, and the end of a task or project is characterised by high mental effort because the goal or task is nearing completion. The amount of mental effort required also becomes clear, and the need for conservatism is reduced as the task nears its end. The middle section is when our mental effort and engagement are most fragile. It's also the middle period when mistakes are typically made, because people are more likely to reduce attention and concentration. The reasons for this dip in mental effort differ somewhat to physical effort. Rather than the brain's desire for homeostasis reining in our physical effort, it is more likely that enthusiasm and novelty wear off in the middle phase of mental tasks.

Overcoming the midterm slump

Understanding how effort changes over time can help us design our hobbies, lifestyle choices and projects to give us the best chance at success. The middle section of an activity is the hardest point at which to maintain effort and engagement. It's like being in a long tunnel where you look back and no longer see the light where you entered, but you look forward and that's just darkness too. In the North American higher-education system, there's a phenomenon known as the 'sophomore slump'. In the United Kingdom, it is referred to as 'second-year blues' and refers to a reduction in motivation, effort and engagement during the middle year of a student's three-year degree. This period is important because students typically report greater thoughts of dropping out during their second year of university compared to their first and last years.[102]

The slump after an initial period of high effort and productivity is not reserved for university students. Similar phenomena can be observed in the dreaded second album in the music industry, or in the second-season syndrome that curses newly promoted teams in football. (Maybe I shouldn't try to write a second book.) If we manage to overcome our initial inertia and start a project, the weak point is unlikely to come during the early phases because of novelty and enthusiasm. A New Year's resolution usually goes well for the first few days. It is even less likely that motivational weakness will occur during the end phases, when urgency and the finish line being in sight become great motivators. If you've managed to get to 4k in your couch-to-5k running programme, or twenty-five days into Dry January, it's unlikely that you'll stop there.

Acknowledging the weak middle section means incentives should be focused during this period to sustain high levels of effort. For example, encouragement from others is most needed during the middle part of a race, not the end or the beginning. If you are a project manager at work, don't worry so much about your team's efforts at the extreme ends of the project. Incentivise and encourage effort during the middle phases. If incentivising effort is not possible, don't put the most important tasks in the middle of a project, as this is when effort wanes. Essential or demanding aspects of your project need to come near the beginning or near the end. Additionally, focus on the softer, intangible motives during the middle section, because they are much more powerful than you think. Evidence shows that people often emphasise tangible incentives like salary and bonuses to motivate and enthuse employees, and not things like interest in the job, staff camaraderie or the importance of the work. But during the hard yards and when the chips are down, it is these intangible, intrinsically valuable aspects of the job that are much more effective at sustaining engagement.[103]

It is possible to take our task modifications a step further by *removing* the middle section as much as possible. Make your tasks small enough that the end of the beginning is the beginning of the end. Just as the energising aspects of novelty and enthusiasm vanish, you will become motivated because the end is in sight. Deconstructing a larger project into smaller components also provides more beginnings and ends, meaning more moments when motivation is high. Instead of focusing your employees' efforts on the finish of a three-month project, insert mini projects that can be ticked off each week – or, even better, each day. I enjoy running, and a five-kilometre Parkrun is about the perfect distance for me to apply this principle. If I'm in good physical condition, I can push my effort at the beginning for about three kilometres, at which point I switch to thinking I'm nearly at the finish and can hold my effort. Any further, and I'd have to include a middle section and regret that I ever laced up my running shoes. Play around with different lengths of task to see which is suitably short for you.

As we approach the end of a task, it is very common to feel stressed about the amount of work still to do. The typical S curve that effort follows over time implies that you shouldn't worry so much. Once you get through the dangerous middle section, effort on the task will almost always increase and allow more progress to be made at the end. Just because you've been completing one section per week on your business-funding application, it does not mean you will continue with this speed of progress as you approach the funding deadline. Your effort will naturally increase, so more sections of the application are achievable in the final week. This idea is applicable to all other tasks, so try to not get too concerned about the amount of work left to do. Your natural increases in effort will bail you out.

The flip side of effort

So far in this chapter, effort has been branded as a nemesis to our dreams and ambitions. At the beginning of tasks, projects and new activities, the human tendency to avoid effort makes it incredibly difficult to overcome motivational inertia. Effort also disappears once the early phases of any activity have been completed, which makes this middle phase a point of weakness in our activities. And yet – the villainous Darth Vader sacrificed himself for the greater good. Apollo Creed developed from arrogant antagonist to lifelong friend of Rocky Balboa. Disney's Maleficent turns from evil dragon woman to warm-hearted curse-breaker. Adversaries turning into comrades makes an appealing narrative. Like these Hollywood rogues, effort has a positive side to its character.[104]

The human tendency to avoid effort typically raises its ugly head when we look forward in time. We avoid opening the laptop because our work project seems too daunting. We don't open the cookbook because we fear the supposed fifteen-minute meal will require three hours of culinary effort. But when we reflect and look back in time, our brains paint a very different picture. Adventurers revel in their arduous continental crossings, climbers admire the difficult peaks they have climbed, and athletes daydream about the brutal competitions they have crushed. We mere mortals similarly look back at effort and see it very differently than we did when we anticipated it. Nowhere can this retrospective effect be observed more clearly than when we self-assemble furniture.

Ninety per cent of the Swedish population, and eighty per cent of Norwegians and Danes, own something bought from IKEA, the largest furniture retailer in the world. These staggering numbers exist despite IKEA's seemingly madcap business model. Many of IKEA's products are unfinished, and the customer needs to build them before they can use them. Would you go to a restaurant where the chef gives you the ingredients for you to create your own meal? A bunch of psychologists consequently wanted to know why people valued products that required effort before they could enjoy them.[105] These same characteristics provide a unique insight into the peculiarities of the human mind.

Imagine being given an IKEA bookcase, the type that comes flat-packed and must be self-assembled. As we now understand, humans typically avoid effort wherever possible, so it's likely you'd prefer it to come fully assembled, rather than having to put it together. However, imagine that a friend of yours receives an identical bookcase ready-made. After you have deciphered the instruction booklet and assembled your own piece of furniture, you and your friend are asked how much each bookcase is worth. You are likely to value your bookcase more highly than your friend does theirs, and this difference can be substantial. When researchers tested this idea with other self-assembly items, such as a simple cardboard box, the average difference in value between the self-assembled and ready-made versions was sixty per cent. The self-assembly group were not willing to pay more because they found the assembly exciting or enjoyable. Nobody thinks IKEA boxes are exciting or enjoyable. Nor were they willing

to pay more because building an IKEA box personally res-
onates with them. The self-assemblers valued the time and
effort that they had invested.

This finding was repeated using origami, the ancient
Japanese art of paper folding. After novice origamists had
designed a paper animal, they were willing to pay three
hundred per cent more for their creations, compared to individuals who were given ready-made origami. The self-made
creations were valued nearly as much as origami created by
experts. Despite wishing to avoid effort, humans paradoxically value time exerting effort.

These experiments were innovative but very tightly controlled, so what about real life? Does this effect occur in
contexts other than furniture assembly and paper folding? We
only need to look at how we spend money to find the answer.
Imagine being in a casino, ready to gamble: the Bellagio casino
in Las Vegas, with its dancing fountains if you're imaginative;
the local dive if you're not. As you approach the entrance to
the casino, you are told that a special promotion has identified
you as the winner of £1,000. In this scenario, you are likely to
spend most, if not all, of your windfall on the blackjack tables
or slot machines. However, if you enter the casino with £1,000
of your own hard-earned money that you've saved over several months, you are more likely to adopt a thriftier attitude.
People who receive a windfall are likely to spend more money
at a casino, compared to those who have earned their cash.[106]
Likewise, individuals typically donate less to charity if they
have earned some spare money, rather than if they are gifted
some.[107] The more time and effort exerted to earn money, the
less is gambled or donated. Money that is effortfully accrued
is more valuable than money that is not.

Running a marathon is an iconic symbol of human effort, one of the toughest challenges in sport. More than twenty-six miles of sweat – and, quite often, blood and tears. For many people, the thought of running such a distance is ludicrous. Given the physical hardship and mental fortitude required to complete a marathon, one might assume that a considerable portion of starters do not finish. But this isn't the case. 54,281 runners started the 2024 London Marathon, and more than 53,700 finished it.[108] This means only around one per cent of runners quit during the race. A typical marathon-training programme starts sixteen weeks before the event, with three or four runs per week. A longer run might take three or four hours for the average runner. Individuals do not typically waste this significant investment of time and effort by quitting the marathon unless they absolutely must. The most common reason for not finishing the marathon is not training enough. In other words, they didn't invest effort in the first place, so there's little to waste if they quit. If time exerting effort was not valued so highly, more marathon runners would fail to finish.

Many more examples exist of the value of time spent exerting effort. A person who fought to be accepted into a clique will like that group more than another who gained entry easily.[109] Cakes taste better if they are believed to be home-made rather than bought at a shop; and cakes bought from a boutique bakery taste better than those from a supermarket. When children obtain stickers for effort, they give fewer away to others, compared to when the stickers are given irrespective of effort. Time exerting effort is valued.

Effort spent is valued to such an extent that we dislike it when we see people being successful without exerting effort.

We prefer people to earn their achievements, and hold others to absurdly high standards of effort. Wolfgang Amadeus Mozart most likely died from illness or disease; however, the popular story is much more exciting. Mozart is often said to have been murdered in a rage of jealousy by his arch-rival, Antonio Salieri. Salieri wasn't jealous over a lover, as is common. He couldn't stand Mozart's seemingly effortless talent. Salieri even struggled with his faith in God because he couldn't comprehend why He would provide such genial musical talent to a spoiled brat who didn't need to work. We've probably all experienced this in some form or another at school. We are often envious of the wonder kid who seems gifted in every sport without so much as a moment's practice. There's always one child at school who fooled around in class but graduated with straight As. These people defy our parents' and teachers' guidance that only those who work hard get to earn the fruits of their labour.

Inspired by the story of Mozart, researchers conducted an unpublished study* to see if this jealousy was real.[110] They asked people to rate several scenarios describing a person with different levels of ability on a fictitious musical instrument called the 'Milano' (good, excellent or world-class) combined with different amounts of practice to get to the level of ability (one hour, five hours or eight hours per day). Participants liked every scenario that included the person practising for eight hours per day, and disliked the scenarios in which the musician's ability stemmed from only one hour of practice per day. In other words, people respected the person when they exerted large amounts of effort, and didn't want them

---

*   The study doesn't seem to have undergone scientific scrutiny from fellow scientists, but it was too interesting for me to ignore

to succeed with little effort. These patterns were reversed when participants were asked to consider themselves as the musician. The scenarios in which they were successful with only one hour of practice were appealing, and they disliked the scenarios in which they practised for eight hours per day. We want our peers to toil for their rewards, but we don't want to have to do so ourselves. This prejudice occurs because we tend to overestimate the price of personal accomplishments but underestimate others' success. We think we moved heaven and earth after running a marathon or starting a new business, whereas it was a walk in the park for others.

Why we value effort remains something of a mystery. Animal experiments have shown that many species sometimes work for food, even though an easy option might be available (except cats; they always took the easy option). This confused scientists, because it went against the idea described earlier in the chapter that all species avoid effort unless it is necessary. The most common explanation was that the animals were making contingency plans. If the easy option no longer existed, they would still need to know how to get food, so they practised the harder option. This idea has since been adapted to humans. It is possible that we exert effort even when we don't need to because we are searching for information about our capabilities and limitations. Some people have a greater desire for this personal knowledge than others, a characteristic called 'openness to experience', one of the five major personality traits that are often described in psychology. People high in this trait look forward to impending effort. Trail runners get excited about heading for the hills, rather than taking the efficient route. Amateur bakers would prefer to hit the kitchen and create instead of eating ready-made pâtisserie. How can we tilt the odds in our favour and be like these winners?

The definition of success

In the late 1970s, four psychologists working at the University of Illinois would meet regularly to discuss their scientific ideas. They were Carol Dweck,* Carole Ames, Martin Maehr and John Nicholls. Born out of these chinwags was the idea that children's definition of success differed at school. Some students measured success by how much they learned and how much they had developed. If they didn't know their maths equations at the beginning of the week, but had learned them by the end, then this was a success. These students defined success by comparing their current ability to their previous performances; what is called a self-referenced definition of success. On the other hand, some students defined success by comparing their performance to that of their peers. If they scored the highest among their friends on a spelling test, then this was perceived as a success. This perspective is a normative-referenced definition of success.

This distinction became widespread in educational research because the two definitions of success were found to predict many important outcomes in students. Students with a self-referenced focus were more intensely engaged with the study

---

*   Carol Dweck also went on to develop hugely influential ideas concerning fixed versus growth mindsets. The former refers to the implicit belief that one's ability is innate and changes little. The latter refers to the implicit belief that one's ability is based on effort and learning and can, therefore, develop over time. Growth mindsets have been associated with far better outcomes in almost any life context you can think of, including work, sport and education settings.

material, and brushed off mistakes or setbacks during their learning. Normatively referenced students would look for shortcuts, and would be more likely to cheat, to avoid challenging tasks because they might look stupid and give up easily.[111] The ideal scenario for these students would be to complete a task with as little effort as possible. Self-referenced students valued effort; normative-referenced students avoided it whenever possible.

Starting in the 1980s and continuing to this day, researchers in many countries have observed that similar processes occurred in sport.[112] Self-referenced athletes work hard to develop and improve, while normatively referenced athletes just want to win to look good, but aren't prepared to risk losing. This is not to say that self-referenced athletes don't care about winning. In fact, a side effect of valuing effort and self-referenced improvement is the tendency to win more competitive matches compared to people who aren't prepared to put in the hard yards. To put it another way, a pleasant side effect of not focusing on winning is winning.

Redefining success also means redefining failure. A fear of failure is one of the most common barriers to exerting effort. Most people are scared to start something new because their ego can't handle failure. By defining success as putting forth the maximum effort, failure becomes defined as a lack of effort. Your effort is one hundred per cent under your control, so success and failure become completely controllable too. The *outcome* of our efforts is often not in our control, especially in competitive situations. You never know when the new Roger Federer or Serena Williams is going to turn up on the other side of your court. Spending months trying to woo a potential client does not guarantee the client will sign with you. A normative-referenced definition of success would mean that you had failed in these scenarios. A self-referenced focus wouldn't.

The importance of these different definitions of success applies to all life contexts, such as work, fitness, hobbies and parenting. In any walk of life, define your success by looking inward. Your focus should be on whether you can improve, try your best during an activity, or learn something new. This self-referenced focus makes it much easier to override our natural tendency to avoid effort, and instead embrace hard work.

In a nutshell

A common characteristic of lost mojo is the feeling of drifting through life without accomplishing anything meaningful. But to initiate a new task or activity is incredibly difficult, and the amount of effort we exert varies according to time. Motivational inertia means that the amount of effort required to get the metaphorical ball rolling is significant. This barrier to our dreams and ambitions is compounded by the innately human tendency to avoid effort. To overcome inertia, we need to break down projects into tiny chunks so that the inertia is appropriately small to overcome. Micro goals also make it much more likely we will experience success, which is a great motivator. Once we have initiated a new activity or project, however, our problems do not stop.

The amount of effort we put into an activity or project over time is warped to resemble an S curve. After the high levels of initial effort have reduced, it is the middle phases of any activity that are the weak point and a danger to our ambitions. We are at risk of giving up on meaningful activities during this time, and any restored mojo will vanish and we'll be back to square one. Efforts to motivate, such as incentives and encouragement, should be focused on these middle sections. More importantly, define your sub-goals and tasks so there is no middle period, and the end of the beginning is the beginning of the end. Finally, define success as improvement, learning and development. By focusing on these motivational ingredients, we are more likely to welcome hard work and toil to meet our goals and ambitions.

8

Home alone

'If you're lonely when you're alone, you're in bad company.'

— Jean-Paul Sartre, philosopher
and decliner of Nobel prizes

After escaping in the wake of his sentencing for armed robbery, twenty-six-year-old Albert Woodfox was recaptured and entered Louisiana State Penitentiary in 1972. Angola prison, as it is also known, is infamous for conditions so brutal that, in 1951, thirty-one inmates severed their Achilles tendon in protest. Along with fellow prisoner Herman Wallace, Woodfox was subsequently convicted of killing a prison guard. Armed robbery and killing guards are typically not crimes associated with lenient prison sentences. And so it was not until 2016, nearly forty-five years after entering prison, that Woodfox was released, on his sixty-ninth birthday. Remarkably, all but two of those years were spent in Closed Cell Restricted, also known as solitary confinement. No phone calls, books, magazines, radios or hot water. When the rats were not around, a colony of red ants were his companions. Frequent anal cavity searches added further humiliation. Even without these atrocities, many of us would struggle to imagine spending forty-three years in a box. In his autobiography, Woodfox described solitary confinement as: 'the most torturous experience a human being can be put through in prison. It's punishment without ending.' According to Amnesty International, Woodfox's punishment remains the longest period of solitary confinement in United States history.

At this point, most descriptions of Woodfox's ordeal would move on to his remarkable tale of resilience and hope. There was defiance in the face of the guards' taunting and abuse, activism about living conditions in the prison, and education of himself and others. He continued to make his bed, clean the walls and mop the floor. His cell became a space to educate, to build morale, to adhere to principles and to maintain health. Woodfox sculpted an unbreakable morality and dignity that no amount of abuse could destroy. Sadly, for every Albert Woodfox, there are a thousand tales of solitary confinement destroying prisoners' souls and breaking their spirits. Individuals playing with their own excrement for shits and giggles, literally. Following a meeting with nineteenth-century solitary-confinement prisoners, Charles Dickens concluded:

'Very few men are capable of estimating the immense amount of torture and agony which this dreadful punishment, prolonged for years, inflicts upon the sufferers ... I hold this slow and daily tampering with the mysteries of the brain, to be immeasurably worse than any torture of the body.'

Society does not seem to have progressed since the Dickensian era. Examples of disappearing dignity, engulfing insanity and deterioration of the human psyche are commonplace. You tend not to hear about these darker cases because their stories do not fit the template of a literary bestseller.

Unsurprisingly, dominant opinion among scientists also condemns solitary confinement as a barbaric and counterproductive measure. The majority think that the evidence of mental and physical decline during solitary confinement is overwhelming. But not every scientist dances to the same beat. Some years ago, Professor Peter Suedfeld, now Professor Emeritus at the University of British Columbia, swam upstream against the flow of opinion. Suedfeld and colleagues interviewed and assessed prison inmates who had experienced between five days and forty-two months of solitary confinement, with the longest unbroken stint a whopping twenty months.[113] What the inmates described was thought-provoking.

Prior to confinement, many prisoners were worried about serious mental and physical deterioration. Who wouldn't be? Everyone is familiar with scenes from TV and film showing confinement at its worst. As anticipated, the first few days were difficult for the inmates, and time passed slowly (another example of time slowing down according to specific circumstances, as described in chapter two). The inmates coped with the monotony by pacing around their cells and trying to sleep more. Despite the inmates' worst fears, erosion of their physical and psychological condition never materialised. They became accustomed to their new dwelling and the absence of distraction. Some prisoners meditated, others fantasised, and some just pondered their current situation. The prisoners began to devote time and energy to understanding their past experiences and contemplating future possibilities. Following their return to normal prison life, they were able to think more deeply, they were motivated to achieve goals and they had an idea of how to accomplish them.

So far, so utopian. If solitary confinement were so idyllic, everyone would be queuing at the local prison or asking to be locked in a basement. Of course, solitary incarceration is far from a dreamy paradise of contemplation. The inmates also spoke of humiliation and abuse, mainly at the hands of younger and less experienced prison staff. Physical beatings and tear gas were common. No educational materials or recreational opportunities; disgusting food and appalling living conditions – it hardly resembled a yoga retreat in Bali. After being released back to their usual cells, inmates reported reduced physical coordination, feeling spaced out, dizziness, eye strain, disturbed sleep and difficulty in re-engaging with their normal routine. The prisoners may have been provided with time to think, but the price was humiliation, abuse and poor health.

And so, surely, we must banish solitary confinement to the history books? Professor Suedfeld took a different perspective by separating solitude and the side dishes that it often came with. Solitude is the experience of being without other people. Confinement is the situation in which a person is kept somewhere, usually against their will. The first word describes a potentially appealing experience; the second describes an atrocity. There is little more soul-destroying than taking away a person's rights. It is the confinement and abuse that is so damaging, not the solitude. Almost all the complaints would be resolved if the guards' behaviour and the poor conditions were removed. Anyone who is abused, poorly fed and made to live in a hell hole will find their body and spirit crushed, whether in solitude or not. Even problems like dizziness, sleep disturbance and trouble engaging with normal routine could be fixed because they largely occurred following *too much* time in isolation and a sudden reintegration into everyday prison life. The prisoners suggested that brief periods of solitary confinement and a gradual reintegration into everyday prison life would negate these effects. If the lighting and furnishing improved, exercise and reading were accessible, and sporadic time out of confinement to test new ideas was permitted, the inmates suggested that solitude could be used for restoration rather than punishment. Abuse and lack of freedom will crush most people, but a regular slice of voluntary solitude seemed appealing, even to people living in prison.

Despite Suedfeld's research programme on prisons beginning in the early 1980s, his perspective on solitary confinement was never widely accepted. This is unsurprising given its potential to ruffle feathers. The mere suggestion that solitary confinement can have positive consequences is likely to raise eyebrows. Admitting that prison systems have turned a blind eye to abuse is also unlikely. But this is missing the point. Suedfeld concluded that solitude can be beneficial *in the right circumstances*. Typical solitary confinement does not classify as the right circumstances. Suedfeld has gone on to lead research in many other areas of life, including polar and space exploration. The conclusions are the same. Solitude can be a friend with benefits.

Why is solitude so good?

The idea that humans are fundamentally a social species is a bedrock of civilisation. Advances from the development of language to the invention of social media are all grounded in the human need to interact. This need is not unique to humans. You only need to observe a herd of elephants or a troop of chimpanzees to see clear social dynamics and structures. Even bacteria can tell when they are interacting with other colonies. But this principle overshadows the fact that the opposite is also true. For every sociable elephant, there's a lone polar bear roaming the tundra (metaphorically at least; in reality, there are fewer polar bears than elephants). For every convivial chimpanzee grooming the alpha, there's a single snake residing in the shade. Humans require time away from our social responsibilities too. Despite several advantages to being social, it can distort our perception of time, create obligation, stunt creativity and prevent exploration.

Examples of individuals seeking solitude are everywhere. In religion, Mohammed regularly settled in a cave on Mount Hira to contemplate. Jesus turned to the desert for forty days of seclusion while resisting Satan's temptation. Moses had a penchant for pitching his tent outside the main camp, far away from others. The creator of Taoism, Laozi (whom we briefly met in the previous chapter), was thought to be quite the recluse. As a result, Taoists believe that solitude is necessary for one's true human nature to develop and provide contentment. One of the pillars of Confucianism is Shendu, which stresses the self-developmental benefits of being mindful when alone. Likewise, fully pledging to Buddhism requires a monastic, solitary life, which is necessary to achieve a true meditative state.

Many artistic, entrepreneurial and political giants have also sought out and advocated for the benefits of solitude. Bill Gates is well known for vanishing for biannual 'think weeks' in his secret cabin in the woods. Barack Obama regularly disappeared into his office alone to shape his future political philosophies and strategies. He also took himself off to an Indonesian island retreat for months to write his book *Dreams from My Father*. Pablo Picasso removed the influences of friends, family and acquaintances to achieve his greatest work. Lady Gaga allegedly prefers solitude, whether she's creating music or just living her life. The writer Samuel Beckett sought solitude for intense creativity to write plays and books, including a period he called 'the siege in the room'. The writer D. H. Lawrence spent much of his later life in solitude, or 'savage pilgrimage' as he called it. The list of solitude advocates across art, science, politics, and entrepreneurship is extensive. In one of the many letters he wrote to his wife while in prison, Nelson Mandela penned this slice of wisdom:

> '... the cell is an ideal place to learn to know yourself, to search realistically and regularly the process of your own mind and feelings ... At least, if for nothing else, the cell gives you the opportunity to look daily into your entire conduct, to overcome the bad and develop whatever is good in you.'[114]

As any recluse will tell you, solitude is so good it can be addictive. From the outset, solitude disrupts your routine which, as described in chapter two, often consists of mindlessly enduring a stressed-out, frantic lifestyle while wearing your busyness as a misguided badge of honour. Disrupting this pointless schedule with a little solitude will interrupt the spiral of negative thoughts and feelings that accompany it. More importantly, time spent in solitude is critical to our spirits, because it removes the burden of other people. It allows us to completely disconnect from family, friends and colleagues. When we interact with other people, be it a trivial exchange with a barista or a deep conversation with a loved one, we automatically consider their experience as well as ours. Social exchanges are always a series of reactions. The way you think, feel and behave is continually shaped by everyone around you. How many times do you smile and laugh, yet secretly you just want to sit in a corner and rest, cry, relax or do nothing? How many times have you acted in the hope of making an impression on someone else? How many times have you reined in your natural reaction, so as not to look stupid, foolish, or angry to others? 'We're all islands shouting lies to each other across seas of misunderstanding,' suggests the writer Rudyard Kipling.

Solitude frees you from these constraints. Self-consciousness ebbs away because you are no longer the object of others' evaluations. You do not have to worry about someone making a detailed assessment of your character based only on the shoes that you are wearing. By diminishing our social obligations and eliminating the demands of other people, we can become free to choose our thoughts, no matter how mundane or perverse. Nobody can tell you what to think during solitude, and you will be amazed at where your brain takes you. You can fantasise, daydream, reflect, plan or recover – the options are limitless. The capacity to be alone with one's thoughts is one of the most important signs of emotional maturity, and is associated with various aspects of psychological wellbeing.[115, 116] Your thoughts in solitude might seem random, but they are not.

The greatest benefit of solitude is so significant that a lesser-known contemporary of Sigmund Freud fought backstabbing and skullduggery to develop previously forgotten ideas on time in solitude that are now revolutionary.

Mention Freud, and you may imagine lying on a couch describing your relationship with your mother or father. Regardless of the myths surrounding Freud, our knowledge of the human mind would not be as extensive without him. Alongside Freud's genius, however, he had a penchant for scheming and manipulation that would have suited any political TV drama. Freud was desperate to remain the alpha scientist of his era, so he established an inner circle of loyal psychoanalysts who would promote his theories and stifle rivals' efforts. Resembling a cult, membership was signified by a ring decorated with ancient carvings of gods and goddesses. In addition to Freud, the group comprised the Welshman Ernest Jones, the Hungarian Sándor Ferenczi, the German Karl Abraham, and the Austrians Hanns Sachs and Otto Rank. The Belarusian, Max Eitingon, was added to the circle in 1919.

Like any good drama, it was not outsiders who posed the greatest threat to Freud's status. Cracks began to appear in the circle when Freud turned members against each other. He separately alluded to members of the circle that each was the most superior intellectual, and jealousy was rife. Ferenczi began to be ostracised for his diverging theories. Eitingon was suspected of being a Soviet agent who helped conduct assassinations around the world. But perhaps the biggest fall-out was with Rank, who left the inner circle in 1924 and was replaced by Freud's daughter, Anna.

Otto Rank was arguably the most dedicated of Freud's inner circle. He was secretary to Freud's psychoanalytic society, editor of several psychoanalysis journals, managing director of Freud's publishing house and a prolific scholar and therapist in his own right. Like other society members before him, Rank began to publish his own ideas that contra-dicted Freud's dogma – and the backstabbing began. Ernest Jones, who'd originally had the idea of establishing the circle, began to publicly shame Rank and claimed his work was the rantings of a manic-depressive psychotic. During a scientific conference, an ally of Freud and Jones claimed that Rank's presentation was simply a confused ramble about his own mental illness. In 1926, Rank had had enough and left Vienna for a new life split between Paris and New York, outside of the psychoanalytic circles littered with deceit, malice and Machiavellianism. So what was so controversial in Rank's ideas that led to other respected scholars indulging in such dark arts?

Rank's views oozed romanticism and imagination. He merged classical psychoanalysis with art, myth and philoso-phy to develop completely new perspectives. Freud and his allies clung to the idea that psychology should be underpinned by biology. If we are mentally ill, we must take a pill or receive a treatment so that we can function better biologically and think 'normally'. Rank rejected this view and refused to categorise individuals as ill or healthy. Instead, his own circumstances and treatment by former colleagues provided a perfect case study of his theories. In a fabulous example of irony, Rank believed social networks that prevent expression of individuals' true beliefs and values are central to the development of illness. Psychological suffering was caused by the individual's creativity and character being stunted by their community, rather than an internal issue that needed to be fixed. From Rank's point of view, a destroyed mojo is largely caused by the people with whom you interact. To reverse this process and rediscover one's true sense of self, solitude is necessary. Inside all humans is the fundamental desire to create their own personality and character, he argued – they just need a little solitude, a little time to become free from the constraints of society, in order to do it. The people, situations and objects we usually interact with only serve to reinforce current identities, not to develop new ones. Your seemingly random thoughts during solitude will help develop and define your character.

At the time, Rank was successfully isolated from scientific communities by Freud and his cronies. The problem was that Rank was way ahead of his time, and Freud excelled at control and dominance. Rank's ideas are now cornerstones of several different fields of psychology. When our minds are occupied with social tasks and interactions, we rarely think about the future. On the other hand, when we are free to allow our minds to wander, most of our thoughts are focused on the future, far fewer on the present, and even fewer on the past. Time in solitude provides a test bed for imagining different identities and future selves. By overcoming our warped fear or neglect of time in solitude, we will become freer to think about what we truly want and who we want to be (more on this in chapter ten). This will lead to new future-orientated possibilities, opportunities and solutions appearing in our minds. People need to spend time in solitude to shape their futures and thrive.

Rank was not the only one thinking along these lines at around the same time. Serbian-American inventor Nikola Tesla held more than three hundred patents for inventions, many of which are still influential today, including the design of the alternating current (AC) electricity supply system. In 1934, Tesla eloquently summed up the benefits of solitude in an interview for the *New York Times*:

> 'The mind is sharper and keener in seclusion and unin-terrupted solitude. No big laboratory is needed in which to think. Originality thrives in seclusion free of outside influences beating upon us to cripple the creative mind. Be alone, that is the secret of invention; be alone, that is when ideas are born.'

Removing any connection with others may seem like a contradiction to our basic desire for social bonds. In prehis-tory, being part of a group meant greater chances of survival and more opportunities for procreation, so it is likely that we evolved to seek out this attribute. Yet, solitude and social con-nection work hand in hand. Knowing we are loved by friends and family can help us unplug from society and head for sol-itude without fear of loneliness. It also works in reverse. In solitude, we often find intimacy. Lord Byron, when not chasing women or fighting wars, labelled solitude as the location 'where we are least alone', and John Milton, the author of *Paradise Lost*, suggested that 'solitude sometimes is best society'. Antarctic researchers often report greater capacity for intimacy following polar solitude.[117] Solitude and sociality are symbiotic.

A great buy, but a tough sell

If spending time in solitude is so vital to our mojos, and people like Albert Woodfox can cope with it for more than four decades, why are many of us terrified of spending fifteen minutes with nobody but ourselves? One of the most astonishing pieces of research in this area reported that a quarter of female participants and two-thirds of male participants chose to subject themselves to an unpleasant electric shock rather than spend a small amount of time alone with their thoughts.[118] Yet, in another study, when students were asked to spend a small period alone, they reported feeling more relaxed, being in a better mood and experiencing little boredom. Although people might go to considerable lengths not to spend time in solitude, when they do, they often discover that it can be therapeutic. Many people's idea of time has become so warped that one of the most valuable ways of spending it seems terrifying.

The reason behind many people's exaggerated fear of time spent in solitude is also its greatest benefit. Unplugging from the burden of others' expectations is horrifying because we can no longer rely on others to determine what we think and do. Many of us live in the service of others' expectations and neglect our own needs and desires. We become accustomed to this inadequate way of living, so we panic when we get a chance to break free. As well as electric shocks in lab experiments, the fear of solitude can get so bad that some lost souls even spend time with people they dislike so they can avoid being alone. Not being able to survive without someone else validating your thoughts, or fearing what your own brain might create for you, is a terrible loss of mojo. The mind has become an uninhabitable place.

If you dislike being alone with your own thoughts, you can point the finger of blame at your parents or guardians. Infants need periods where they explore alone, but with a caregiver in the background to provide support only if necessary. If the caregiver is too attentive, then the child does not develop the ability to thrive in solitude and relies on others to guide their thoughts, feelings and behaviour. When the child grows up, this inability manifests as anxiety and loneliness when alone, and the easiest coping strategy is to avoid the experience and to seek social interaction. This tendency to avoid unpleasant situations is called 'experiential avoidance' and is another one of many safety mechanisms from prehistory that are no longer fit for purpose. For our ancestors, emotions like anxiety signalled that we were in danger, and something needed to be done. This was essential when we slept in the savannah and needed to avoid carnivorous beasts.

Nowadays, life-endangering situations are rare, but the emotional signals remain. Reacting to these emotional alarms even though there is little threat of real harm is counterproductive. It makes us fragile and lacking resilience. We have very few direct sources of pain and danger, yet humans tend to suffer greatly at the hands of our own thoughts and feelings. Ironically, the more we attempt to avoid difficult thoughts and emotions, the more influential they become. Trying to avoid anxiety will only make it more of a feature in your life. This is why owning a video doorbell is completely counterproductive. Many people are anxious about house security, so buy a video doorbell in the hope of making it less likely that they will be burgled. Not only is there no evidence to suggest that video doorbells reduce crime, but having the ability to constantly monitor your front door is also unlikely to do any favours for your anxiety.[119] We buy them, nonetheless.

We need to dive in, accept that solitude might sometimes be uncomfortable and reap the rewards. As well as anxiety, you may feel lonely when in solitude, but it is loneliness that is the problem – not solitude. Some anxiety and negative feelings are normal, but they are just feelings. If something is troubling you, then solitude provides the perfect environment in which to ponder and find potential solutions if you can give it time. The French Nobel Prize nominee Colette described solitude perfectly:

'There are days when solitude is heady wine that intoxicates you, others when it is a bitter tonic, and still others when it is a poison that makes you beat your head against the wall.'

Embrace all that solitude brings in the beginning, good and bad.

Some people might think that embracing time in solitude is lazy, but they would be wrong. Laziness is idly killing time and filling your attention with pointless distractions like showbiz gossip despite more valuable alternatives being open to you. Hopefully, these periods were removed after reading chapter two of this book. Time in solitude is about creating an environment that allows your mind to wander. Cast your mind back to when you last had a creative thought or figured out a solution to a problem. This might be very difficult, if not impossible. For those who can, I'm willing to bet it didn't occur while you were scrolling social media.

The different faces of boredom

As well as our warped perception of time creating a fear of being alone with one's thoughts, solitude is avoided because many people fear boredom. There is little doubt that boredom has an image problem. British photographer Sir Cecil Beaton once claimed that:

'Perhaps the world's second worst crime is boredom. The first is being a bore.'

But the reality is more complex.

Air traffic control is a well-paid occupation for good reason. When airports are at their busiest, traffic controllers need to act fast, with precision and clarity, hundreds of times every hour. During the quieter night shifts, they must remain vigilant and prepared at any given moment. It is often these quieter times that pose the greatest risk of error. If you were flying your plane over Ohio one night in April 2011, you may well have heard audio from the film *Cleaner*, starring Samuel L. Jackson. The night shift was quiet, so an air traffic controller decided to watch the blockbuster instead of his dashboard. I doubt that he's the first shift worker to watch a movie during the quieter, boring moments of shift work. A good friend of mine used to do this during his job on the London Underground. However, this unfortunate air traffic controller also had his microphone switched to the transmit position, so everyone could tell what he was up to. More alarmingly, this switch position also prevented him from receiving incoming radio calls from pilots. He was only alerted to his misdemeanour by a military pilot who used a different communication system.

Aviation is not the only profession characterised by fluctuating periods of boredom and hyperfocus. Anaesthesiology is often described as ninety-nine per cent boredom and one per cent panic. Watching paint dry is a real and important job for paint manufacturers. Many night workers and people in jobs that require being on standby will experience a lot of boredom, too.

Boredom can also infiltrate leisure time. In 2018, a man tried to alleviate his boredom by stealing a Russian tank and driving it into a supermarket.[120] A survey of two thousand adults by the British Heart Foundation found that the average British citizen spends five years of their life feeling bored.[121] In an extensive study of nearly four thousand adults in the US, scientists asked participants to report their feelings every half-hour during waking periods for ten days.[122] Nearly two-thirds of the participants reported being bored at least once during the study period. Boredom is not the sole property of humans, either. Researchers study boredom in animals to answer important questions, like how much land a cow needs to prevent boredom, and what a chimpanzee needs to be entertained in their enclosure.

Whether boredom is a new thing depends on your historical perspective. The ancient Roman philosopher Seneca wrote about people who are plagued with indecisiveness and distraction, and compared them to people who 'loll and yawn'. Similar acknowledgement of boredom-like tendencies can be found throughout ancient literature, but the word only came into popular use in the eighteenth century. Anglo-Franco relations were not at their strongest at the time, and to be 'in a bore' was an English phrase referring to the uniquely French ability to have a dull time. It wasn't until 1853 that the word 'boredom' officially entered the *Oxford English Dictionary*.

The term gained popularity as a generic term, rather than a French barb, because industrialisation led to rising free time for many people. This worried the middle and higher classes, who thought that the working class wouldn't know what to do with their free time and might succumb to boredom. Commoners would undoubtably engage in all manner of immoral acts if they were bored; therefore, they needed to be policed. Following World War II, men and women returned to their family roles and were supposed to fall back into the supposedly ideal family archetype (male breadwinner, house-wife and their children), but new technology and new cultural ideas had changed everything. Boredom was still pictured as dangerous, but no longer just for the working classes. What if women got bored at home because the washing was so much easier? Would they also get bored of their marriages? What if young people got bored outside of school? Would civilisation fall into a pit of depravity?

Boredom is typically highest in children, and tends to decline in the late teens and early adult years, possibly because brain development is nearing its optimal point and there's more freedom to take advantage of, such as being able to drive and drink alcohol (not simultaneously).[123] Low levels of bore-dom typically continue until the late fifties. During this middle phase, a lack of boredom largely stems from parenthood and not even having a moment for basic personal hygiene, never mind the time to be bored. When people reach their sixties, boredom starts to rise again (especially in women, for some unknown reason). During this period, brain function declines and many of life's responsibilities, such as parenting and a career, slow down and begin to disappear. Boredom will increase if these obligations are not replaced with activities of personal value. Boredom also varies according to your personal circumstances. A recent study on humans aimed to identify the most boring person in the world (hypothetically, of course).[124] Participants were asked to list stereotypical jobs, hobbies and living locations of boring people. From over three hundred jobs and hobbies identified as boring, the researchers found that a data-entry worker who slept a lot and lived in a medium-sized town was the most boring person. Apologies if that description fits you.

Because boredom is largely viewed as undesirable, most scientific attention is given to preventing the negative consequences of boredom. People who are prone to frequent or long periods of boredom are more likely to suffer from depression and anxiety, as well as struggling with drug abuse, excessive alcohol consumption and gambling. Chronic boredom may also increase your stress levels and subsequent cardiovascular disease. In a survey of more than seven thousand US civil service workers, those who reported high levels of boredom were thirty-seven per cent more likely to have died by the end of the study. It's likely that boredom led people to take up unhealthy habits, such as poor diets and excessive time spent being sedentary.[125]

In 2021, a quirky group of researchers from Europe and the US made half of their experimental participants bored by having them engage in a repetitive and monotonous task.[126] The other half watched an interesting documentary about the Alps (the participants were German, so likely had some affiliation with the Alps). Both groups were then given the option of killing maggots by shredding them in a modified coffee grinder. The three maggots were given names (Toto, Tifi and Kiki) to humanise them and to make killing them a sadistic act. Only one person shredded worms following the Alps documentary (perhaps they had a penchant for beach holidays rather than mountain getaways), whereas nearly a fifth of the bored participants shredded at least one maggot. Boredom increased sadism.*

Despite these negative consequences of boredom, we needn't be afraid of it during periods of solitude. Different types of boredom exist, and some are more useful than others. Sometimes we are bored because we want to do something else, but don't know what. Even worse is an apathetic type of boredom where the feeling of helplessness is combined with no desire to do anything about it. Some boredom can also lead to frustration or anger, which only makes the situation worse. None of these types of boredom are what we are looking for during solitude. We are searching for an acceptance of boredom, where we embrace boredom for what it is, understand that it will pass in time, and take advantage of the chance to reflect, reboot, daydream and be creative.

A similar perspective was described by the German writer Siegfried Kracauer. In his 1924 essay on the social consequences of increased technology and modernising factory work, he described two types of boredom. The first type refers to the drudgery of everyday life and a diminished sense of individuality. The second type he called 'radical boredom', which meant reflecting on the social norms that bombard us and oppress us. Why can't we wear that outfit? Why can't we hopscotch down the street when we are forty years old? Why

---

* You will be glad to know that no worms were harmed thanks to a secret modification in the coffee grinder.

can't we look at our business opportunities from a different perspective? Why can't we change our lives for the better? Kracauer viewed radical boredom as offering huge political potential because it can lead to ideas that shape future society – but there's no reason why we can't seek radical boredom in moments of solitude for personal gain and to shape our future lives. Even before Kracauer, melancholy was often viewed as essential in order for poets and writers to produce their best creations. The Irish writer Anne Enright suggested she wouldn't have been able to write award-winning books without this positive form of boredom:

'Boredom is a productive state so long as you don't let it go sour on you. I wait for boredom to kick in because boredom, for me, is a very good sign.'

Despite these benefits of boredom, we frantically search for some other activity that will alleviate it. We often reach for our mobile phones, in the hope that scrolling through social media will eradicate this form of boredom. Unfortunately, people typically report increased fatigue and boredom *after* having used their smartphone to cure boredom. Scientists in Canada also found that, when people were bored, they continuously fast-forwarded and flicked through digital content, rather than immersing themselves in what they were viewing. The people they studied believed that this would help reduce their boredom, but it actually increased the tedium.[127] Do we need to avoid boredom when in solitude? No – we need to embrace radical boredom.

The logistics of solitude

So go for a walk, sit still, lie down, look up at the stars – whatever flicks your switch. Just do it alone. Ensure that thinking, not doing, is the dominant activity. Too much physical or mental effort spent on a specific task does not allow your mind to fulfil its creative potential. There are many benefits to being immersed in a novel or painting a future masterpiece, but these activities are not what we are seeking right now. If you're having difficulty listening to the thoughts inside your head, then writing them down can be a great way of working through and evaluating those thoughts and emotions later. Going for a walk is a great activity to embrace solitude, as long as it's a safe environment. If it's not, there'll be too much background activity as your mind scans for potential threats to your safety. After a few minutes of strolling safely, the mind will wander. If something is on your mind, it'll stick around and be tackled by more creative thought processes than those we experience outside of solitude.

Running is often viewed as an opportunity to think things through, but its relationship with solitude can be complicated. In the previous chapter, low-effort running was advised to increase the likelihood of sticking to it longterm. A low-intensity run can also allow for creative thinking, but if the physical effort gets too much, it will then take up too much attention and impede the benefits of solitude. Running enthusiasts often speak about different zones of intensity. Zone one is for recovery and physical adaptation. Zone two is a slightly higher intensity, but you should still feel comfortable and be able to easily hold a conversation. These two zones allow for the creative benefits of solitude to occur. Any higher, and the mental demands of the exercise will dominate. It's very surprising how easy these zones should be; for many people, anything more than a brisk walk is too intense.

The place of solitude also requires some consideration. Participants in an experiment were asked to engage in solitude for several minutes in a city garden or in a university seminar room. Both environments led to a significant increase in relaxation, but participants were more aware of their surroundings and thoughts in the city garden.[128] Renting a secluded lodge like Obama and Gates may be financially beyond many of us, but we can all find somewhere different from the norm. For many, it is in nature where solitude is found. A forest, a beach, a lake, a river or a hilltop are particularly agreeable venues for solitude, but any outside space might be suitable. Train journeys are one of my favourite opportunities for solitude. Nobody wants to speak to me or cares what I am thinking. I rarely hook up to the Wi-Fi, so the time spent travelling is my own. Travelling by car does not offer the same opportunities for solitude, because you are frequently disturbed by the clown up your ass or having to decide which turn to take.

It is possible to experience solitude at home, but I would not recommend it. Your home reinforces your current thoughts and feelings, so it is very difficult to let your creative juices flow in the place that bolsters the norm. The shower might be an exception because people often relax in the shower, or just taking a walk around the block can give you a sufficient break. Get away and let the mind flow. Finally, this might be stating the obvious, but mobile phones do not lend themselves to constructive solitude (which is another reason why having a shower might work).

In a nutshell

Solitude is essential if you are to unplug from your current physical and social relationships, which only maintain the status quo. By adding a little time in solitude to your life, you will become free to think and feel how you want. Despite these benefits, many people's beliefs on how they spend their precious time has become so warped that they would do almost anything to avoid solitude. It might take a few attempts, but once your mind has freed itself from the social shackles, the creative juices will flow. Many of the clichéd 'Eureka!' moments occur during solitude. Scientists are alone when the solution pops into their minds. Painters and authors create their masterpieces in solitude. Researchers working in the extreme solitude of Antarctica frequently comment on their ability to concentrate, to become completely absorbed in their tasks, and to imagine and fantasise with startling clarity and vividness. Solitude enables the imagination to create different scenarios, visualise about potential realities and evaluate which ones might appeal and be effective. Solitude is the psychological fitting room where you can try on alternative ways of living, thinking, feeling and doing, without the pressure to buy. Solitude will help you develop more insight into who you are as a person. Removing social pressure allows you to focus on your true self, not who you think others want you to be. All these benefits are critical to restoring your mojo. These processes cannot occur when you are busy or when the expectations of others are weighing you down. A slice of time and a dash of solitude are two major ingredients for a healthy spirit. In the words of Roman Emperor Marcus Aurelius:

*'For nowhere can you find a more peaceful and less busy
retreat than in your own soul … Treat yourself often to
this retreat and be renewed.'*

9

Rose-tinted glasses will never go out of fashion

'Memory can change the shape of a room; it can change the color of a car.'

– Leonard Shelby, completely fictitious
film character from *Memento*

On 8 November 1979, the owner of an antique store in Gretna, Louisiana, was raped at gunpoint. Four months later, police reports describe the victim as 'tentatively' pointing to a photo of a man named Malcolm Alexander. Three more days passed, and the victim 'possibly' identified Alexander in a police line-up. Later that day, a detective took a statement describing the victim as 'ninety-eight per cent' sure that Alexander was the assailant. At the time of the trial, the victim testified that she had 'no doubt' that Alexander was the attacker. Alexander was not helped by having an awful attorney who failed to appear at court, neglected to call any witnesses, and didn't even make an opening statement (the attorney was subsequently disbarred). A guilty verdict was passed.

Some years later, two attorneys called Peter Neufeld and Barry Scheck discovered they had mutual interests. As well as their training in law, both had a strong affinity for civil rights, but more importantly, they both understood the power and potential of science. Neufeld and Scheck founded the Innocence Project in 1992 to use DNA and other cutting-edge scientific methods to prove wrongful convictions. In 1996, they took on Malcolm Alexander's case. Over the course of their investigation, they discovered that crucial evidence had been wrongfully destroyed, and other evidence not appropriately examined. Hair samples from the crime scene did not match Alexander's profile, nor that of the victim. In 2018, after thirty-eight years in prison, Malcolm Alexander became the Innocence Project's longest-serving exonerated client.[129]

This story illustrates several human and systemic flaws. According to the Innocence Project, inaccurate eyewitness identifications contributed to over two-thirds of the 375 convictions overturned by DNA evidence in the United States.[130] Eyewitnesses are expected to use their memories to identify offenders, which is like using marshmallows as the foundations to your house. Alexander's conviction also arose from numerous factors that alter memories from 'tentative' and 'possible' to being 'ninety-eight per cent sure' and having 'no doubt'. Alexander was the only person who was included in the photo identification and police line-up. The three days between the two procedures blurred whether the witness recalled the person in the line-up as the perpetrator or the person from the photo they'd been shown. These distortions were compounded by the fact that the accuracy of witness testimony is typically worse when weapons are involved, probably because the witness is focusing on the weapon and

not the perpetrator. Any hint of pressure, accidental or delib-
erate suggestion, or simply a delay between experiencing an
event and recalling its features will lead to difficulties when
the eyewitness attempts to accurately recall events.

Most people understand that memories can fade, but this
is only part of the story. The legal example above demonstrates that memories can strengthen or adapt over time. Each
retrieval of a memory makes the brain networks associated
with that memory open to modification over time. It is almost
impossible to overestimate how malleable the human memory
is. In 1990, Gary Ramona was a high-flying vice-president for
a Californian winery. His daughter, Holly, entered counselling for bulimia and depression, and was told by her therapist
that bulimia was usually caused by incest and sexual abuse.
Holly began believing that this was what had happened to
her, and agreed to take sodium amytal to help recover any lost
memories. Later that year, she confronted her father, claiming that the memories were triggered when her father made a
sexual suggestion during the previous Christmas. Gary lost
his family and job, but, in a complex trial, he became the first
person to successfully bring a legal case against a medical
team for allegedly implanting false memories.

This case, and others like it, brought the fragility of human
memory into the mainstream consciousness. An analysis of
US popular media reported that, in 1991, four out of five articles on childhood sexual abuse were favourable towards the
survivors. Three years later, the trend had reversed, with four
out of five articles questioning the accusations, the memories
of the abused and the therapeutic methods employed.[131]

The scientific basis of repressed and false memories is
equally as muddled. Scholarly thinking in the nineteenth

century was led by hypnosis experts, such as the founder of modern neurology, Frenchman Jean-Martin Charcot. Imaginatively nicknamed 'the Napoleon of the neuroses', Charcot's startling medical legacy includes advances in diagnosing multiple sclerosis, tooth decay and joint degradation. Another of Charcot's major ideas was that distressing events can be unconsciously repressed and blocked from entering the conscious mind, so that people no longer recall them. These memories do not disappear totally but instead reside in unconscious memory, which means that they can still have mental and physical consequences. To treat these symptoms, it is necessary to transfer the traumatic content from the unconscious to the conscious memory.

Clinical professionals accumulated numerous examples of this process when working with patients who had experienced trauma and repressed it. In the 1980s and 1990s, thousands were coming forward in the US claiming that they had recalled memories of abuse during Satanic cult rituals. This period has been dubbed the 'Satanic Panic'. According to those who believe in repressed memories, survivors only remember the abuse when it is psychologically safe to do so, potentially many years later. Ordinarily, people would remember a traumatic event, like a car crash, because it is psychologically safe to do so. Abuse is different if you still feel threatened. In other words, the brain protects the individual by repressing the abusive experience. Significant portions of the public also think that repressed memories are possible. In a survey of two thousand Norwegians, nearly half believed that traumatic memories can be repressed in the same way that Charcot had suggested.[132]

This explanation was largely dismissed by scientists,

sparking a rift called 'The Memory Wars'.[133] Traumatic events are not always perceived as traumatic at the time they take place. It is uncomfortable, yet necessary, to consider that a child, for example, might not know that what is happening to them is so abhorrent at the time. This means the suggestion that trauma is repressed as a defensive mechanism must be false, because the event wasn't perceived as traumatic. Instead, it must have been simple forgetfulness that doesn't occur as a defence mechanism. Likewise, why is the human mind's ability to repress trauma so ineffective, with many people remembering their trauma? Wouldn't it be more beneficial to keep the memory repressed? Although firm conclusions on the existence and function of repressed or false memories remain out of reach, these endeavours have significantly advanced our understanding of how the brain creates, stores and adapts memories.

Imaginary rabbits and a drug-fuelled dog

It is not surprising that our brains make mistakes when trying to recall events. Long-term memories are not stored in one section of the brain. Memories are first captured in the hippocampus, which then sends different aspects of the memory to other parts of the brain. For example, words are sent to the temporal lobe, whereas the emotional aspect of the memory is stored in the amygdala. The memory of going to a bar is composed of the people who were there, the smells, the music that was played, the physiological sensations created by the bar, and so on. If someone asks you about this experience, then your brain almost immediately retrieves each aspect from different parts and integrates them into one memory. This disparate storage makes it unbelievable that memories of whole episodes can be recalled with any accuracy at all. Give the brain a break if it makes a mistake every now and then.

The complexity of how the memory functions makes it very simple to modify memories. English psychologist Frederic Bartlett first examined memory adaptation in the 1920s and 1930s. He asked his English participants to read and then repeatedly recall the Native American folktale, 'The War of the Ghosts'. Over time, the details of the story became more and more distorted to fit with the participants' own English values and histories. For example, the 'canoes' morphed into more general descriptions of 'boats', and 'hunting seals' became 'fishing'. Bartlett's work provided the basis for distinguishing between incorrectly recalling information and actively modifying information. Once scientists knew that our memories could be actively shaped, they created increasingly wacky experiments to test it.

Bugs Bunny, the flippant cartoon rabbit with a Brooklyn accent, was integral to many childhoods. He also helped researchers discover how easy it is to alter memories. A group of US scientists provided participants in an experiment with a mock advertisement for Disneyland vacations based around Bugs Bunny.[134] The participants were subsequently asked to recall their childhood memories of visiting Disneyland. After seeing the advert, three-quarters of participants were more confident that they had shaken hands with Bugs Bunny, and sixteen per cent of participants firmly remembered doing so. These memories were nonsensical because Bugs Bunny is a Warner Brothers character and has, very likely, never set foot in Disneyland.

That's not all folks. Mickey Mouse's pet dog, Pluto, represents the only one of Disney's 'Sensational Six' (the others being Mickey and Minnie Mouse, Donald and Daisy Duck, and Goofy) to behave like a real animal and not have significant human characteristics, beyond a few frowns and smiles. Participants in an experiment were asked several questions about Disneyland, including whether Pluto had ever licked their ear.[135] Almost all the participants confidently claimed that Pluto did not lick their ear. A week later, half of the participants were told that a person who played Pluto at Disneyland had abused hallucinogenic drugs and inappropriately licked the ears of children in the 1980s and 1990s. The other half were told that Pluto was lovable and sometimes delighted children by playfully licking their ears. Thirty per cent of participants who learned about the wicked Pluto, and thirty-nine per cent who were given the lovable Pluto scenario, now reported a solid memory of him licking their ear.

A cartoon rabbit appearing in a cartoon theme park is plausible, as is a cartoon dog pretending to lick your ear. A group of researchers from the UK and Netherlands raised the stakes to demonstrate how easy it is to create completely implausible memories in the minds of young children.[136] The research team rang up the parents of ninety-one primary-school children (aged between seven and twelve years old) to gather some basic details about the child's first day at school, such as who escorted them to the school and the name of the teacher they met first. Armed with these facts, the researchers interviewed the children about their first day at school. In half the interviews, the children were asked about choking on a piece of candy, which was plausible but false. The other children were asked about being abducted by a UFO. The researchers sometimes used fake newspapers to add credibility to both stories.

When the newspaper wasn't shown to embellish the UFO story, over twenty per cent of the children remembered being abducted by a UFO when asked. When the newspaper was used, more than three-quarters remembered being abducted by a UFO – and a week later, two-thirds still remembered being abducted. The number of children who did not see a fake newspaper but remembered being abducted rose from twenty-one per cent to around a third of the participants a week later. The memories did not significantly dissipate over time; in fact, they got stronger in some children. This trend is consistent with other research demonstrating that false memories sometimes strengthen over time. Even after the researchers told the children that the event was false, nearly forty per cent remained convinced that it had occurred.

These brainwashing effects are not solely reserved for the fallible minds of children. The same group of researchers successfully inserted a hot-air ballon ride into the memories of young adults. Other false memories implanted into per-fectly sane human beings include getting lost in a shopping mall, knocking over drinks at a wedding, being bitten by an angry dog, getting a finger stuck in a mousetrap, receiving a rectal enema and committing theft. Psychologists do not lack imagination. Sometimes, the grander the false story is, the more likely it is to be memorised. Being accused of copying at school was more easily implanted into memories of experimental participants than simply moving to another classroom.[137]

Not all participants in experiments develop false memories, but the numbers who do are significant. In some investigations, up to seventy per cent of participants created a false memory, although the overall rate tends to be a little lower. When a study included an aid to make a story more believable or relevant, like the newspaper describing a sudden increase in UFO abductions, nearly half of participants typically developed a false memory. It's worth remembering that these studies commonly employed a brief experimental suggestion that led to new memories, sometimes of the most extravagant or unbelievable events. Outside the research laboratory, our own minds have much more time and opportunity to create delusions than any experimental manipulation, especially if the modifications to our memories are plausible.

There are several ways in which memory can be altered. Simply imagining something has happened can develop into a real false memory. In an experiment based in the UK, some participants were told to imagine having a nurse remove a skin sample from their little finger, while other participants were simply asked to read about it. Those who imagined the medical procedure reported greater beliefs that it had occurred, and nearly thirty per cent were steadfast in their memories of the procedure. The only problem is that this medical procedure is never performed in the UK.

Memories can also be created when similar things have been remembered. This process has generally been investigated using different words. When experimental participants read related words, such as 'candy', 'sugar' and 'taste', they also often remember reading the word 'sweet', even though they haven't. Similarly, when a person reads 'soldier', 'gun', 'camouflage' and 'war', it is common to add the word 'military' when asked to recall the words that they read, even though it was never on the list.[138]

A third type of memory distortion occurs when false information is given which helps modify the memory of the event. In an experiment, participants watched a film with others and completed an individual test about the film. Four days later, some participants received fabricated answers supposedly given by others in their group while some did not. The participants who received fake answers were more likely to remember aspects of the film that never happened.

These methods of memory distortion are scientifically interesting, but do not tell us much about how to raise our spirits, find our mojos and make us view life in a positive light. We could imagine that we haven't felt sad, anxious or burnt out in the past, in the hope that we erase these memories, but this sounds like psychobabble. The fact that we falsely remember similar words doesn't have any practical benefits for our wellbeing. Getting people to provide us with fake information isn't pragmatic. Fortunately, there's a fourth and more straightforward method: let time do its work.

Rose-tinted glasses

Our faulty memories can see people being wrongly convicted of crimes; they can distort memories of abuse, and create all sorts of implausible experiences. When artificial intelligence developers in the 1980s were considering what to base their models on, they dismissed the human mind because it was so inaccurate and unreliable. However, the scepticism surrounding the flakiness of human memory is misleading. The malleability of memory plays an essential role in maintaining our wellbeing. Thankfully, perceptions have moved on, and the flexibility of human memory is now viewed as an exceptional advantage. Artificial intelligence tools, like ChatGPT, contain networks called transformers, which are modelled on neuron connections in the brain that help explain how memory and other brain functions work. Viewing the pliability of human memory in a positive light provides an opportunity to use it to maximise our wellbeing.

Although it is sensible to assume that accurate recall of events is preferable, a totally objective memory would probably destroy our wellbeing. Memories of our past need to be constantly updated to align with our developing values and attitudes, and social norms, all of which make up our core sense of self or identity. If our memories of the past stayed rigid, they might become irreconcilable with our current values, which would create serious psychological discomfort. Time alleviates this distress by modifying the memories of our actions to align with our new attitudes. An individual might believe they are kind and generous but, in the past, did something harmful to another person. Aspects of the harmful event may be altered or removed from the memory to avoid conflict with their 'kind and generous' persona and reduce psychological distress. If the memory of the event remained the same, then the enduring conflict between the person's actions and beliefs would cause considerable harm, and the 'kind' persona would be damaged. A malleable memory is necessary to protect our own identities.

Imagine that some years ago, you dithered around in an important work meeting with the big bosses and could not come to a firm decision quickly. Now, things have changed, and you believe that you are an effective decision-maker. The memory of the meeting fiasco would sting because it misaligns with your current beliefs. In instances like this, time will help alter your memories of the meeting. You might create a mitigating factor, such as a colleague providing inaccurate figures on which you were told to base the decision. Continually recalling the meeting allows your brain to further adapt the memory. You showed great delegation skills by allowing a colleague the opportunity to make the final decision. You were the definition of an effective corporate leader. Our memories and identities are so integrated that individuals with significant amnesia often have trouble describing and reflecting on their core values and true character.

In addition to protecting our identities, our adaptable memories can be employed to our advantage by changing how we *feel*. Many of us chuckle when reflecting on school romances and broken teenage hearts. Getting dumped by your first real boyfriend or girlfriend no longer makes your stomach contort with sorrow. The brain can go a step further and delete feelings from our memory entirely. My good friend hated every minute of our cycling trip to the French Alps; he even considered deliberately crashing in the hope of breaking a bone, just so he didn't have to cycle anymore. A few years later, he feels nothing but fondness for the journey. Time provides us with a shiny pair of rose-tinted glasses. Our emotions and feelings are accurate for a fleeting moment, and subsequently evolve into total fallacies. If we allow time to work its magic, our memories of thoughts, feelings and behaviours, no matter how dreadful at the time, can be shaped and manipulated into something more palatable for the soul.

Silence is golden

If we possess an amazing mental system that adapts our memories over time to maintain our identities and erase negative feelings, why is poor health so common? Unfortunately, giving ourselves the gift of time is unfashionable, and other, quicker methods of sustaining our mojos and raising our spirits are often advocated. Modern dogma universally demands that you must not suffer your negative feelings alone – 'It's good to talk,' after all. Social media invites us to share our thoughts and emotions, and reminds us of them on their anniversary. Communicating our sadness and sorrow releases pleasurable and rewarding hormones. The sympathy we often receive from listeners also soothes us. These physiological and psychological benefits provide a short-term tonic, so we are motivated to reveal our misery and gloom again and again, even though it comes at long-term cost.

Adopting these approaches to positive mental health is often counterproductive because the adaptation of memories requires the magic ingredient of time in order to function effectively. A memory becomes solidified through two processes, namely *retrieving* it from long-term memory storage with the intention of using the information, and consciously *rehearsing* or repeatedly going over the memory. Communicating your transient feelings and moods to other people requires you to engage in both processes, making the memory enduring and objective. If you tell a friend that you committed a shameful act, then the act will remain shameful for longer. Your friend's memory will not seek to change the event, because it does not risk contradicting their personal beliefs. Your friend's future interactions with you will be based on the knowledge that you felt ashamed, making the shame linger even more. Instead of the cheery greeting you usually receive from your companion, you get: 'I hope you're OK; how are you feeling now?' You proceed to discuss the whole episode again, which requires further retrieval and rehearsal. Collaborative remembering has been shown to strengthen memories beyond individual recall,[139] so the solidification of your memory of a shameful act is further enhanced. Your friend might try to reassure you (rightly or wrongly) that you have nothing to be ashamed of. This support may offer some comfort, but it rarely effectively changes your perceptions of the event.

Nobody did anything wrong in this scenario, and your companion seems like a lovely person. Chatting to your friend may help you get over the shame eventually, but the approach you employed made it much more difficult than necessary. In contrast, if an experience is not rehearsed through communication, memories adapt quickly. Within a much shorter period, you'll no longer remember the incident as shameful, or you might find yourself able to justify the act. The association between communication and strengthening memories is why historians rightly argue that it is ethically essential *not* to be silent about war, otherwise we will not recall the atrocities accurately and mistakes will be repeated. Communication to improve our mental health rarely provides the same benefits.

The same delays in memory adaptation and healing can be created by posting your feelings on social media. Unlike your memory, the words that you type online do not change over time. Attempts to communicate your mood online in a futile attempt to change it only halts the process. Maybe social media companies could emulate our memories and allow posts to disappear over time to reduce the conflict between our past feelings and present self. Until this functionality is created, it might be worth periodically deleting old posts that are no longer a reflection of your memory. Otherwise, time's healing power can be delayed by you seemingly doing the right thing and expressing your feelings.

Talking about how downbeat we are may provide some short-term benefits, and is fine if the social support is *always* there for you. But what if it isn't? Other people have their own problems to deal with, or changing life circumstances might make it difficult to rely on others. This is a common occurrence observed in overprotective parents who do not provide the opportunity for their teenagers to mope in their bedroom for a couple of days after being dumped or dropped from the sports team. When they flee the nest, how are the children supposed to deal with their normally fluctuating mental health without the parents' intervention?

Instead of trying to communicate our worry and gloom in the false hope of ridding ourselves of them, a different approach is to apply a business principle from the land of the rising sun. Japanese business meetings are often interspersed with periods of silence. If, after a sales pitch, Japanese business associates remain silent, it usually means they dislike the proposal, and the offer needs to change. Put simply, the Japanese fill time with silence to instigate change. We can apply the same tactic to boost our psychological health.

Silence in its various forms is often an underrated experience. It can lower blood pressure, heart rate, breathing rate and the stress hormone cortisol. In quiet hospitals, patients recover quicker and are less stressed, and preterm infants tend to develop better. The arch nemesis of silence, noise, is one of many factors explaining why urban citizens are more likely to develop mental disorders compared to rural dwellers. To allow our memories to adapt and lift our spirits, we need a specific type of silence. Silence in this context is much more than the absence of sound, which has very little implication for our memories. Some psychologists call it mnemonic silence, which is the refusal to speak out while acknowledging that content exists in your memory. For example, you may recall an event and feel down about it, but you don't speak about it. This acceptance signifies to the brain that some aspect of the memory might need to be changed, and it gets to work.

The phrase 'suffer in silence' is very rarely used nowadays to describe a positive act. It often means the wrongful toleration of abuse, bullying or injustice. It can mean suffering clinical disorders and loneliness without seeking help. The evolving conversation around mental illness over the last few years has largely crushed the idea of suffering in silence. But, if you are free from mental illness, and are simply feeling anxious, stressed or downbeat, try giving your memory time to heal your soul. Time continually alters memories and can be a wonderful soother – if only we would let it. To be clear, this is not a suggestion to stay silent when something unlawful or cruel has happened to you. The appropriate people need to hear about events like these as soon as possible. Nor is this a rant against a 'snowflake' mentality or a suggestion that everyone should stop whining that they are depressed. If you are suffering from depression or another clinical disorder, then you need to speak to someone, ideally a professional.

Silence was not always so unfashionable. Mnemonic silence has considerable overlaps with aspects of Stoicism. First developed by ancient Greek philosophers around 300 BCE and exported to imperial Rome, Stoicism is experiencing a renaissance in the twenty-first century. Stoics believe that living according to the four virtues of wisdom, moderation, justice and courage is all that is necessary to live a contented life. This viewpoint implies that a Stoic is psychologically resilient to adversity and suffering because these conditions have no bearing on happiness. Stoics also believe that the best indication of an individual's true beliefs are actions not words. Combining this perspective on resilience and diminished reliance on verbal expression implies that we often do not need conversation or words to tackle hardship.

It wasn't just the ancient Greeks who rated silence. The phrase 'speech is silver, silence is golden' has been around in the Arab world since the ninth century. Christians typically take Jesus as their role model, and what did He do? Did He grumble when He was betrayed? Did He complain when in agony? Did He proclaim His innocence? No, Jesus suffered in silence. Suffering in silence was not viewed as an act of hopelessness, but of belief. It was not necessary to verbalise anguish to get God's attention. A respectful silence was advocated as the response to pain or suffering. To 'suffer in silence' meant letting time soothe your soul without the need to chat about it.

In some countries, there's little option but to suffer in silence. The anthropologist Michael Jackson lived and researched in the villages of the Kuranko people in Sierra Leone. Over the period of his fieldwork, Sierra Leone experienced famine, war and many other tragedies. Here's an extract from Jackson's paper 'The prose of suffering and the practice of silence':

'It is difficult to do justice to what people suffered in the
Sierra Leone conflict, but one may perhaps venture to
describe how people responded to their suffering. And here
I would like to emphasize something that struck me years
ago, living and working in Kuranko villages—the way
people are taught to accept adversity, and endure it. It is
the overriding lesson of initiation, when pain is inflicted on
neophytes [people new to the experience] so that they may
acquire the virtues of fortitude and imperturbability. Pain
is an unavoidable part of life; it can neither be abolished
nor explained away; what matters most is how one suffers
and withstands it.'[140]

In the US, a nationwide survey asked more than seven hundred older adults how much they sought out emotional support
during financially stressful periods.[141] People who spoke to
others about their troublesome money situations reported
symptoms of depression during times of financial strain, such
as poor appetite, restless sleep and lack of energy. Those who
suffered in silence showed no symptoms of depression. It isn't
always good to talk. Older Catholics tend to be particularly
adept at suffering in silence because it was taught as the only
appropriate response to pain and grief. Another US survey
discovered that Catholics were less likely to seek emotional
support from church members during periods of moderate
stress compared to Protestants.[142] Only during periods of
high stress did Catholics seek the same amount of emotional
support as Protestants. This finding implied that the Catholics
sought emotional support from others when their psychological health was at its lowest. For the general ups and downs
of life, they remained silent and let time massage their spirits.

This approach seems to be effective for many people. During lengthy interviews with more than fifty Mexican Americans, most of whom were Catholic, several participants noted that suffering in silence empowered them in different ways.[143] Suffering in silence helps people feel that they are not a burden to others, and allows them to maintain independence. Why would you want to burden others with your burdens? Suffering in silence helps you become stronger in the knowledge that it is possible to cope when similar things come round again. Suffering in silence may also allow you to discover other coping strategies that you didn't know that you had available to you. On the flip side, relying on others to soothe your soul prevents you from developing internal protection and resilience.

I'm not suggesting we all copy Jesus and subscribe to Catholicism, but we can learn a few things about how to live well from biblical tales written by respected scholars and philosophers. Admittedly, some of these tales have aged better than others, but if you dismiss the more persecutory fables, then you can discover the occasional piece of wisdom. Contained within the book of Proverbs, King Solomon tells us:

'Who so keepeth his mouth and his tongue, keepeth his soul from troubles.'

– Proverbs 21:23

Paradoxically, knowing that emotional support is there if you need it drastically reduces your need to seek it and break your silence. In other words, there is a significant difference between having an emotional support network and receiving emotional support. The latter can sometimes increase depend-ence and subsequently reduce self-esteem.[144] The former acts as a safety net that provides you with the confidence to work through problems on your own. Based on this distinction, your strategy should be threefold. First, ensure that you have a social network to access if you *really* need it and you need to reach out for help. Who are the friends and family you can count on when the chips are down? Second, make it very clear to your loved ones that you are there for them if *they* really need it. Third, take on the responsibility of looking for signs that your loved ones might need you. The balance between sucking up some emotional distress and seeking help from others is a delicate one, and it's often difficult to make the right choice. It's often easier to make the decision for your friends than for yourself. Has their behaviour suddenly changed? Are they failing to make work or social commit-ments? Do they look healthy?

In an imaginary world where everyone adhered to these rules, we'd all have the confidence to tackle our issues on our own by letting time soothe our souls. Improving our mojos in this way would free up resources to provide a support net-work for others while they work through their own issues. And when life did spiral beyond the general ups and downs of life (which it will), we would all have a network to reach out to and help us ride out the bad times.

In a nutshell

Despite having been called 'a little arsehole' by an influential critic early in his career, Luis Buñuel is widely considered one of the most influential filmmakers of all time. In his memoir, he wrote about memories being much more than a place to store experiences.

> *'You have to lose your memory, if only in bits and pieces, to realise that memory is what makes our lives. Life without memory is no life at all ... Our memory is our coherence, our reason, our feeling, even our action. Without it, we are nothing.'*

Buñuel was correct. Our memories shape our identities and our feelings, but they are also fallible. Our brains can erase, strengthen or create completely new memories, even ones of being abducted by UFOs or licked by drug-fuelled cartoon dogs. This ability has its drawbacks, but also provides us with an exceptional method of preserving our mojos. Uncomfortable thoughts, feelings and actions that may have occurred in the past but no longer align with our current values and beliefs can be massaged and manipulated. For this to happen, we need to give ourselves time, and not try to force our negative emotions on other people by communicating with them. Time in silence has a long history in therapy, psychological research and religion, but suffering with our own thoughts and emotions is no longer fashionable and is often derided. Nobody should view suffering alone as their *only* option. But the ability to stay silent about feelings is an essential tool for optimal living. Dealing with emotional adversity on your own can strengthen coping strategies when adversity arises in the future. More importantly, it gives time the chance to work its magic on our memories. Follow in the footsteps of Greek politician Pericles who believed that 'time is the wisest counsellor of all'. Hold your tongue, bite your lip, put a sock in it.

Human beings not human doings

'One's real life is so often the life that one does not lead.'

– Oscar Wilde, unsurpassed provider of quotes

Every year, thousands of teenagers finish school and disappear on a gap year before entering work or going to university. The often-derided aim of this trip is to find their true self, or to discover who they really are and who they want to be. A gap year might be unfeasible for many of us (although vagabonding across the globe is an exciting idea) but developing who you are, in the deepest sense, should be a central principle that guides your life. It is often said that 'there's no magic bullet' that will solve an individual's poor mental health and related problems. There's no single solution to the rising tide of anxiety, depression and stress many people face. Understanding who you truly are – and who you want to be – and letting that guide your everyday actions comes close to being the magic bullet. Our core identity is the long-term solution to many of the problems that time sends our way that have been described earlier in this book. Spending time defining and living in line with your true identity is the essential and final ingredient for finding your mojo and developing a rewarding relationship with time.

Identity is an abstract and vague idea. When psychologists use the term, they could be referring to a variety of characteristics, such as personality traits, attitudes, beliefs, goals or social relationships that make an individual unique. This unclear definition can be confusing, especially for those who do not often contemplate who they are and what they deeply value (which is most people, I suspect). In practical terms, an effective way to determine your identity is to select a handful of labels that you would use to describe yourself to others. These labels could be something you do as work, such as butcher, baker or candlestick-maker. They could also reflect your major relationships, such as being a mother, father, son or daughter. Alternatively, these labels could also represent a defining feature of your character, like 'confident', 'laid-back', 'stubborn' or 'resilient'. Any label is appropriate if it truly defines who you are. A 'unicycling, anarchic bon viveur' would be a great identity, but the labels don't have to be as theatrical as this. A 'healthy-eating, loyal, coffee-loving father' would be a perfect identity too. If you try this activity, hopefully you identify mostly positive characteristics, but don't be afraid to acknowledge the occasional weakness too. 'Forgetful', 'cantankerous' or 'disorganised' are fine, but don't stray too far into self-deprecation and label yourself an 'evil, hateful dictator' (unless you tyrannically rule a country and oppress your citizens). If you struggle to identify some characteristics, or can only recognise functional aspects of your life that don't mean much to you, then work on developing some defining features during your solitude (see chapter eight). Spending some of your well-earned time identifying the labels that make up your identity is useful because, whether you know it or not, they significantly shape the way you act, think and feel.

Answer the following philosophical question with a yes or no answer:

Do you feel free to express who you really are?

If the answer is 'yes', I'll bet that you are reasonably content and happy with the world and your life. If it's a 'no', then this conflict has significant repercussions for your wellbeing. One of the primary causes of psychological illness is a clash between how you are living your life and your core identity. A significant amount has been learned about this process by engaging with the LGBTQ+ community and their experiences of 'coming out'. Although many people still use the term, it is gradually being replaced by the contemporary term 'disclosure'.

It's easy to think of disclosure as a one-off event where Lady Gaga's 'Born this Way' belts out, party poppers explode and everything changes. There's the occasional funny story found online. When a son revealed that he was gay, his dad replied, 'I had sex with your mom,' because he thought they were playing a game of stating the obvious. Another person allegedly said to their aunt, 'I think I'm gay,' and she replied, 'OK, call me back when you know.' However, it's more accurate to think of disclosure as a transitional process that occurs over time. It can be a daunting process for many people, which nonetheless provides the opportunity to begin behaving in line with one's core identity. Non-disclosed individuals do not have this prospect. Deciding whether to disclose is often a catch-22 situation. Concealing one's true sexual identity may well protect you from the significant stress of discrimination and mental ill-health, but not living in line with your core identity is stressful, and is also associated with mental ill-health.[145] If we remove discrimination, then the decision to disclose becomes more straightforward. Indeed, positive disclosure experiences tend to be the privilege of those who are socio-economically advantaged because less discrimination is experienced.[146] A summary of nearly two hundred scientific studies revealed that concealing one's sexual orientation was associated with more mental health issues, such as depression, anxiety and disordered eating.[147] In contrast, when individuals were interviewed about their disclosure, their mojos improved in several ways. Some people felt more authentic, others developed meaningful relationships, and others became more aware of societal issues.[148]

The LGBTQ+ community provides a context where individuals often move towards aligning their identity and behaviours by disclosing their sexual identity. In the world of elite sport, the reverse process often happens. Athletes behave in line with their significant athletic identity by eating healthily, training hard and resting when appropriate. And then retirement happens. In an interview with the Canadian Broadcasting Corporation following her retirement from figure-skating, Kaetlyn Osmond, world champion and Olympic medallist, described herself as feeling 'like a boat adrift at sea', and spoke about her identity troubles:

'Mentally, retirement is difficult, because you lose a large part of [the] identity you've had your whole life.'[149]

In fact, Osmond's issue was that her athletic identity still existed, but she couldn't live her life as an elite athlete anymore.

Many athletes live and breathe the athletic lifestyle, so it is unsurprising that many of them struggle after retirement. Their identity remains athletic, but they no longer get up at 5am to train, they no longer interact with fellow athletes, they are no longer the centre of the crowd's adoration. There's also the daily grind of hours spent in pain and discomfort during training. Athletic retirement is different from other retirements in that it is often the beginning of a second career, rather than the end of work altogether. In this second career, athletes might have to act like 'normal' people, and sit at a desk or report to managers on a regular basis. This misalignment makes retired athletes susceptible to experiencing depression, alcohol and substance abuse, eating disorders and many other problems adjusting to their new lives.[150] Even in Olympic athletes, a misalignment between identity and actions causes significant distress. If it can happen to them, it can happen to you.

We are our goals

The concept of identity has been contemplated by the greatest philosophers for millennia, and scientifically investigated for well over a century. However, a significant amount of our understanding about human identity has stemmed from the intellectual work of two men. The first started out as a young boy called Erik Homburger, who was born to Danish parents, grew up in Germany, and was raised as Jewish. He grew up as a tall, blond, blue-eyed boy who ate kosher. Erik was bullied at his Jewish school for being Nordic, bullied at grammar school for being Jewish, and changed his name to Erik Erikson when he started at Yale University. In hindsight, it's not a huge surprise that he coined the phrase 'identity crisis' and developed one of the most influential theories of identity. He believed that our identity never stops developing throughout our lives and, while an identity crisis can be traumatic, it also represents an opportunity to psychologically grow.

The second major scholar of identity was William James. The American psychologist, whom we met briefly in chapter two, deliberated extensively on the features of identity. He described identity as being composed of three parts, including the 'spiritual self', representing core values and beliefs, the 'social self', representing interactions, and the 'material self', referring to things owned. This division underscores that we have a core sense of who we are, and this can be expressed by what we have, what we do and who we do it with. James suggested that the spiritual self is the bedrock of our identity and shapes all other selves and behaviour. These philosophical ideas turned out to be more than musings, because these different identities have been subsequently shown to be related at a neurological level. When people think about these different aspects of their identities, the same part of the brain is activated (the ventromedial prefrontal cortex, should you be interested).[151] Nowadays, scientists who study the link between identity and behaviour often use different terms to those that James coined. Rather than talking about different selves, it is common to focus on the goals that people value most. A major feature of your identity is the fundamental goals that you strive for.

Some types of goals are explicit, like 'start a business', 'save money' or 'run a marathon', but there are other more subtle, implicit goals that are equally important in determining our behaviour. For example, most people do not overtly think about the impression that they are trying to present to others on a moment-to-moment basis. Social interactions would be very disjointed if every sentence you spoke was preceded by actively thinking about the best impression to give. Instead, the goal to present ourselves in an appropriate manner quietly directs our interactions in the backgrounds of our minds to make conversation more seamless. Many other implicit goals exist, from the basic drive for survival to desires to acquire social status or demonstrate power. Every single action we take has an underlying goal behind it, no matter how small and beyond our conscious awareness it might be. Actions without reason would be a complete waste of energy and resources; something which is contradictory to our basic desire to conserve energy (a point that was made in chapter seven). Implicit goals may not be part of our conscious thinking, but it doesn't make them less important.

Not all goals are created equal. Goals vary in their ability to motivate, initiate and, more importantly, sustain behaviour. Different goals are stored in the brain hierarchically, a bit like keeping them in a chest of drawers.[152] In the top drawer are the most powerful goals, which are broadly aimed at keeping us alive. If you haven't eaten all day, for example, then the goal of satisfying your hunger will dominate your thinking and shape most of your behaviour. If a truck is hurtling towards you at fifty miles per hour, then the likely goal for the next few seconds is to get out of the truck's path. All other goals can wait a little longer until these goals are met. For good reason, these basic survival goals will always be in the top drawer (unless you have severe psychological illness), and we don't want to interfere with this fact.

All other goals can be broadly separated into three categories. In the lowest drawer are 'have' goals, such as the goal to *have* a new car, to *have* more money or to *have* a better body. These goals share many similarities with the material aspects of the self that referred to 'things owned' described by William James over a century earlier. In the next drawer up are 'should' goals, which reflect doing things to align with social obligations and standards. These goals overlap with James's social self. Aiming to visit your slightly weird uncle, which you don't *want* to do, but you feel like you *should* do, is an example of this type of goal. The important element here is not *what* you aim to do (visit your uncle) but *why* you are doing it (because you feel you *should* do it). Finally, sitting just below the drawer containing survival instincts are your 'be' goals. The aspiration to *be* an exerciser, to *be* an entrepreneur or to *be* a great friend are all examples of 'be' goals. These goals resemble James's spiritual self, and refer to the desire to act out our core values and beliefs. If one of the labels that we have given ourselves is 'bookworm', then we will want to fulfil our goal of being a bookworm by voraciously reading books. In other words, 'be' goals are the motivational component of our core identity. This categorisation can help us understand how to stick to dreams, plans and ambitions, because these diverse goals are weighted differently in the brain. 'Be' goals have a huge motivational weight and are valued much more highly in our brains than other goals.[153] This power makes them very effective in helping you to persist and sustain your actions. In contrast, 'have' and 'should' goals possess less motivational weight and are not sufficient to power and sustain behaviour in the long term. Spending time creating 'be' goals will pay dividends.

There are two important characteristics about human identity that explain why 'be' goals are such a potent motivation. The first is that all humans are inclined to demonstrate their identities so they can form bonds with like-minded people. This act was essential in our evolution, because having better relationships meant having a better chance of surviving and copulating. The best way to communicate your identity to others is through your behaviours and the things that you do. Whether you're aware of it or not, your identity drives your behaviour. 'Be' goals are the part of your identity that facilitates this process. If you identify as healthy, then you'll be motivated to behave in ways that communicates healthiness to others. In other words, you want to *be* healthy. If you identify as a maths geek, you'll be motivated to behave accordingly and want to *be* a maths geek. Possessing 'be' goals is an essential human process, because they allow us to express our identities.

The second important aspect of human identity is that we want consistency between our behaviours and the core attitudes and beliefs that make up our identities. American psychologist Leon Festinger is well known for infiltrating a doomsday cult and conducting research on what happened when a prophecy of Armageddon on 21 December 1955 didn't come to fruition. Unsurprisingly, the most hardened believers proposed that it was their complete devotion to the doomsday idea that made God spare Earth from complete annihilation.

A few days later, the group, called The Seekers, began to publicise a new prediction. Spacemen would travel to Earth in a flying saucer and take them to outer space. As far as I'm aware, this has yet to happen.

When Festinger turned his attention to philosophising about identity, he theorised that any discrepancy between our behaviour and the deeply held beliefs that make up our identities is psychologically uncomfortable.[154] If someone with strong beliefs about protecting the environment buys a coffee in a single-use plastic cup every day, then they are very likely to be irritated or annoyed with themselves. This psychological discomfort motivates us to resolve the discrepancy between beliefs and behaviour. One way to resolve this discrepancy is to modify one's behaviour to fit one's identity. In the environmental example, the person might eventually buy their own reusable bamboo cup and bring that to the coffee shop every day, so that their behaviour conforms to the belief that they are environmentally friendly.

An individual's identity is such a potent motivational influence that actions that don't conform with it are often modified until they do. Put simply, your identity is like a dictator.

This influence also explains why changing behaviours that we want to rid ourselves of is often difficult. If you have a 'lazy' identity, for example, then getting up early to start work will conflict with it, and your brain will encourage you to modify that behaviour until it aligns with your lazy identity. In cases like this laziness example, we want to do the opposite by sustaining the desired behaviour and modifying the less-than-ideal identity over time. This is difficult, but not impossible, to accomplish. We will return to this possibility later in the chapter.

The tendency to express your identity and the need to resolve conflicts between identity and behaviour can be applied to numerous examples. For example, identity plays a central motivational role in a person's choice from the lunch menu. There are two choices on today's menu. Option one is some grilled fish and salad shipped from across the Atlantic Ocean. Option two is a locally sourced chicken and mushroom pie with potato dauphinoise. Health Nut Holly and Eco Ellie are perusing the options. Holly is more likely to be attracted to the grilled fish option, because she has a desire to express her healthy identity, and taking the other option would create a discrepancy between beliefs and behaviour. Ellie will likely be drawn to the locally sourced produce as a display of her eco-friendly identity. Choosing the fish, with its extensive carbon footprint, would create internal conflict.

The identity is such an important motivational system that the brain makes choices like this automatically and constantly. Holly and Ellie's decisions would likely not be made deliberatively nor overtly, and very little decision-making effort would be required. Why waste time and risk their conscious brains messing things up?

You don't know it, but your brain is constantly scanning for opportunities to express your identity and to identify inconsistencies that need rectifying. It is difficult to describe subconscious brain activity in words, but imagine you are deciding whether to go to a language class or not. One of the first questions your brain will ask is: 'Does going to this class fit with a core component of my identity?' Put another way: 'Does going to the class allow me to *be* a multilinguist?' If the answer is 'yes', then it is difficult for alternatives or obstacles to get in the way of going to the class. This process occurs for all behaviours, not just virtuous or worthy ones. If you are relaxing, watching Netflix, and deciding whether to open the second tube of sour cream and onion crisps, the brain will ask, 'Does bingeing on crisps fit with a core component of my identity?' If the answer is 'yes', then the crisp tube gets popped. If the answer is a definitive 'no', then a discrepancy between your identity and the behaviour is recognised and corrective action initiated. The crisps are more likely to be stored for another day.

If the potential behaviour that is under consideration neither aligns nor conflicts with core identity, it doesn't have any implications for achieving 'be' goals. The brain will then progress to evaluating whether the behaviour achieves less important 'should' and 'have' goals. These lower-status goals are motivationally inferior to 'be' goals and no match for the tricks played by time described in this book. For example, 'have' and 'should' goals typically require significant amounts of willpower, which we know from chapter three isn't a good thing. These inferior goals are usually temporally disconnected from the actions that are needed to fulfil them, which we know from chapter four is a mistake. It takes a long time for any meaningful progress towards 'having' a better body to occur from changes in diet and exercise. This time gap between action and goal was highlighted as a motivational weakness in chapter five. These lower-ranked goals are motivationally weak in the face of obstacles and alternatives, and do not lend themselves to achieving dreams and ambitions.

'Be' goals bypass these human flaws and are impervious to the dangers of time. *Being* an exerciser requires less willpower than doing exercise to fit in with others. *Being* a geek is easier than studying to obtain good grades. *Being* relaxed is simpler than trying to relax because everyone else seems relaxed. For these reasons, 'be' goals should be your motives of choice, and spending time defining them will work wonders for your mojo. Being healthy, more productive, or content with one's life is an unfair business. Healthy people find it easy to be healthy, productive people find it easy to be productive, and contented people find it easy to be contented. For the rest of us, it's very difficult.

There are several features of 'be' goals that make them particularly potent. First, the drawer in the brain that contains 'be' goals can be accessed easily and only needs a nudge to slide all the way open. Any seemingly insignificant trigger in the environment can activate a 'be' goal and provide an opportunity for it to be realised. In contrast, the drawers containing 'have' and 'should' goals are stickier and harder to open. These inferior goals are not activated in the same way. For example, the desire to demonstrate a healthy identity, or 'be' healthy, is likely to be activated in the brain when the option to take the stairs rather than the escalator presents itself. In contrast, a person wanting to lose weight to 'have' a better body is less likely to notice the stair option. The desire to demonstrate a caring identity, or 'be' caring, will be activated when a frail person is holding on to a wall during strong winds. A person who thinks they 'should' care because society demands it is less likely to notice the frail person. 'Be' goals bias our attention towards stimuli that provide opportunities to express it.

Those annoying office cabinets that require you to shut one drawer to be able to open another provide a good analogy for another characteristic of 'be' goals. Once the 'be' goal drawer has been opened, the other drawers beneath it become difficult to open. Our brains dedicate much more attention to pursuing 'be' goals, which means that little attention is left available for other, lesser, goals. *Being* healthy means walking down a street full of fast-food joints without paying much attention to them, even if it might be nice to eat a burger. In contrast, possessing a weight-loss goal to simply align with cultural 'skinny' ideals will not skew attention in the same way. This inferior motivation means that considerable attention is available to notice those fast-food delights and succumb, despite this 'should' goal of wanting to lose a few pounds. Healthy people do not live in a different dimension where there are fewer obstacles to being healthy; they simply notice fewer obstacles than people who do not possess a goal of *being* healthy.

Another feature that explains the power of 'be' goals is that they are much more resilient to inevitable setbacks. To use a phrase by Iain Dowie, cult football hero from the 2000s and ex-Premier League manager, individuals driven by 'be' goals have greater 'bouncebackability'. When trying to achieve some goal or ambition, it is very rare that progress is faultless. Runners get injured, investors back the wrong stock, a student receives a poor grade. These setbacks can be a momentary lapse in judgement, such as succumbing to a sweet indulgence, or a broader failure, like losing a contract to a business rival. 'Be' goals are a manifestation of your core identity and values, so they are difficult to give up on following a setback. Instead, individuals driven by 'be' goals are more flexible and responsive to setbacks, whether that takes the form of altering a strategy for next time, or dedicating more attention, effort and resources to the activity. Someone who holds running as a core part of their identity will work hard on their rehabilitation following injury. The investor will reflect on the reasons for their losses and adapt for the next investment. The student will digest the feedback and improve next time. All this leads to more likely goal achievement in the future.

In contrast, it is much easier to give up on lesser goals because they do not represent who you are, and so are less important. Individuals motivated by these inferior goals are more likely to exaggerate the consequences of temporary failures and perceive them as permanent failures. In other words, the wheels will come off your dreams and ambitions very easily. An individual who wants to start running because their group of friends has started running will be more likely to give up when they get injured. The investor who's desperate to have a lavish lifestyle will likely start to chase their losses and make more ill-advised investments. The student who wants good grades to please their parents will probably start to skip revision sessions.

The art of brainwashing

'Be' goals can be used to motivate from a very young age. Parenting, for example, involves spending at least six hours per day tidying up after your little cherub after they have obliterated the living room. But hope is at hand. In a scientific experiment, groups of four- and five-year-olds were split into two groups.[155] The first group were told that some children choose to help, and they could too. The second group were told that some children choose to *be* helpers, and they could *be* a helper too. These instructions are subtly different. The first set of instructions used a verb ('to help'), while the second set used a noun to activate a 'be' goal ('*be* a helper'). Both groups of children were then given four opportunities to help tidy up while playing with new toys. Children in the noun ('be' goal) group helped tidy three times out of four, on average, while children in the verb condition helped tidy just over half the time. For good measure, the researchers replicated this experiment in a different sample of children and found the same effect.

Similarly, labelling children with the personal characteristic 'neat and tidy' encouraged them to conform to this label more than simply asking children to tidy up.[156] Offering children the opportunity to *be* helpers rather than *to* help will give you a tidier house. An identical effect is also observed in adults. In a psychological study, when adults were labelled 'helpful', they were more likely to volunteer in their communities, compared to participants who weren't labelled.[157] The same effect occurs if you say something nasty to someone. Calling someone a cheater is more meaningful than saying that they are cheating.[158] Tell someone that they are a liar will likely produce a bigger emotional response than telling someone that they are lying because the former criticism suggests lying is part of their character.

Given the allegations of political vote-rigging in the 2020 US presidential election, the results of another scientific study are intriguing, albeit a little worrying in their demonstration that voting behaviour can be manipulated so easily. Researchers sent out a survey to California residents who had not yet registered to vote in the 2008 presidential election.[159] Approximately half of the residents received a survey with questions like: 'How important is it to you to *be a voter* in the upcoming election?' Like the previous experiments, using a noun ('a voter') in the survey was designed to activate a 'be' goal for these participants. The other half received questions including verbs, such as: 'How important is it to you *to vote* in the upcoming election?' Citizens who received the noun-based 'be' goal survey reported being much more interested in voting, compared to those who received the verb-based survey. Just before the election, the researchers sent the same two surveys to people who had registered to vote. Data obtained from official records revealed that ninety-six per cent of participants who received the noun-based 'be' goal survey voted, compared to eighty-two per cent of participants in the verb group. A simple change in wording to activate a 'be' goal seemingly increased voter turnout. The researchers repeated this trick in the 2009 New Jersey gubernatorial election. Ninety per cent of participants who received the noun-based 'be' goal survey voted, compared to seventy-nine per cent of participants who received the verb survey. Something as seemingly innocent as a postal survey can activate 'be' goals and energise action. Shift people's identity by emphasising 'be' goals and they are likely to start conforming to the label. It's like mind control, but lawful.

These scientific studies demonstrate the possibility of changing the behaviour of others through self-fulfilling processes. If you want someone to be kind, tell them how kind they are. If you call someone a profanity, watch how they miraculously start acting like your choice of profanity. Perhaps the most famous philosopher of all, Aristotle, wrote in his treatise *Rhetoric*: 'to praise a man is in one respect akin to urging a course of action'. Hypnotising or blackmailing people might be effective, but these methods tend to come with some side effects, like a prison sentence. Instead, try complimenting an aspect of their character associated with what you want them to do and watch what happens.*

This wordplay also provides an opportunity to reduce unwanted thoughts and behaviours. If undesirable behaviours are characterised as part of one's identity, they are likely to be consistently expressed and sustained over a long period. For example, people who describe themselves as being 'stressed-out' are unknowingly setting an unwanted 'be' goal. This label suggests that it is part of their character to be stressed and will, therefore, drive much of their behaviours. Instead of *being* stressed, try to recast your view of an event or period in life as stress*ful*. This externalises the problem and does not attribute the stress to your core sense of self. Doing this consistently for unwanted attributes will help you disentangle them from your character and live your life for the better.

The dark side of identity

Up to now, identity has been portrayed as the magic motivational recipe we've been looking for. It would be more accurate to portray identity like the Infinity Stones in the early Marvel Universe films. Identity's motivational power can underpin fantastic transformations, but in the wrong hands, it can support all sorts of ill-judged acts. Humans also develop darker aspects to their identities, meaning 'be' goals can also direct people towards misguided actions. If your identity in the form of a 'be' goal involves *being* a criminal,

---

* To all readers, thank you for being such a flattering and generous reviewer of this book.

then it will make criminal activity more likely. Someone who is characterised as *being* a bully will require very little effort to behave like a bully. If you continually cheat on romantic partners, then your identity will move towards *being* a cheat and make being unfaithful more likely next time. All the processes described in this chapter can work in negative ways too.

This sinister side to identity explains why it is very difficult to halt negative acts if they stem from one's identity. A person who views smoking as part of their identity (rather than just someone who smokes) may seek to minimise internal conflict by viewing the world in a biased way. They may underestimate their chances of getting lung cancer. They'll probably say things like, 'My nan smoked twenty a day, and she lived to a hundred.' An unbiased perspective would view their nan as an anomaly, not the norm. Smoking increases the probability of spending your final days bedridden and having very little say over when you go to the toilet. Those who identify as 'being a smoker' will likely have little desire to quit and will not have paid that last sentence much attention. Your identity shapes what you focus on, what you believe in, and what you do every day.

Your identity can also cause problems if different facets clash. Having multiple components to your identity is healthy because it provides flexibility and protects overall self-worth if one aspect of identity is compromised. In risk-management, having a single point of failure is to be avoided at all costs, and your identity is the same. For example, if your whole identity is based around your work and then you retire, then the transition is likely to be very challenging.

This problem would not exist if you had multiple parts to your identity. For example, imagine two parts of your identity are being healthy and being sociable. You intend to go to the gym on Thursday evening, but a few work colleagues are going for a burger and a few drinks to celebrate meeting their monthly targets. You're tempted by this soiree, so hit the town with your colleagues and skip the gym. The next morning, your healthy identity is compromised, but this issue is mitigated because your fun and sociable identity is validated. This adaptive psychological flexibility is only available if you possess multiple sides to your identity, although it sometimes comes with its own challenges. *Too much* conflict between your different aspects creates a lot of unhappiness. For most of the time, the different facets of your identity need to be flying in the same formation. It is worth considering how your different aspects complement or antagonise each other, and figuring out how to solve the latter, if necessary. It might be that the sociable aspect of your character could be fulfilled in different ways that do not conflict with the healthy aspect of your character. Alternatively, it may be that you embrace the unhealthy but fun behaviours at certain times during the week, and at other times the healthy identity takes precedence.

To be something, you must do something

Many people think that your identity doesn't change over time, which implies that 'be' goals are similarly fixed, especially when you reach a certain age. *You are who you are. You can't teach an old dog new tricks.* Do not be fooled by these phrases. In the words of executive leadership coach Marshall Goldsmith: 'What got you here won't get you there.' Your identity may not be as flexible as your thoughts, moods and emotions, but it can be adapted over long periods, and new aspects can be added. Think of the reformed criminal who is now a shining role model for the youth of their community, or the lazy person who hated anything to do with physical education in school and now runs marathons. Who you are or who you were are not necessarily who you can be.

The fact that identity can be moulded provides a great opportunity to shape how we tackle the rest of our lives. The importance of dedicating time to solitude was championed in chapter eight for exactly this reason. You need to spend time thinking about your new reality – specifically, who you want to *be*. This does not mean going back to a child's state of mind and dreaming about being an astronaut, a professional athlete, or a singer (although there is no harm in doing this). Spending time creating 'be' goals is about developing a set of core values and beliefs that shape your everyday behaviours.

Any reputable company has a vision that guides employee behaviour. 'Be' goals are your personal vision. Many of the world's most successful companies also have 'be' goals as their mission statement. The mission statement of McDonald's is 'to be the best quick-service restaurant experience'. Disney aims 'to be one of the world's leading producers and providers of entertainment and information'. Sony desires 'to be a company that inspires and fulfils your curiosity'. A company mission statement focuses different areas of their business into one coherent strategy. Otherwise, each department will focus on their own areas and have incoherent goals.

The same can be said about individual 'be' goals. They allow different areas of your life to align and work towards the same aims. For example, being environmentally savvy allows you to walk and cycle instead of driving, but it also allows you to buy locally sourced food in the weekly shop, to identify with people who share common ideas and values, and to spend less on fast fashion, which simultaneously looks after your finances. Just like company mission statements, individual 'be' goals provide direction and focus, and help align all your behaviours in the same direction.

Perhaps you already have some goals in mind, but they are not associated with a desired future identity. You may want to start a business, for example. This is a worthy goal, so it shouldn't be dismissed just because it isn't a 'be' goal. Instead, the goal could be adapted from 'start a business' to 'be a successful businessperson'. This latter goal is broader in scope and provides a vision around which several more concrete life goals can align.

Once a company has set out their vision, the corporate-education powerhouse Harvard Business School suggests that a strategy to realise the vision should be mapped out. They further recommend that business leaders link their strategy with tasks. This step allows employees to see the value in what they are doing, because they can see how they are contributing towards a specific business goal. In the same way, we need to understand how our 'be' goals are expressed as behaviours. Identify what actions would constitute successful 'be' goal progress. Having specific behaviours that express a 'be' goal allows you to be very clear on how you need to act. To *be* something, you must *do* something.

For example, imagine your 'be' goal is to be a great parent. The next question is, 'What do great parents do?' This sets out the strategy for how you are going to realise your vision. These behaviours don't have to be grand gestures, but they do have to be specific. In my case, the answers to this question would be centred around paying attention to my daughters. A great parent puts their mobile phone away when their daughters are around. They also turn off the TV, and they sit on the floor or get to the same level when they play with their children. These behaviours may mean absolutely nothing to other parents, but that is missing the point. Not only are 'be' goals unique to any individual, but their expression is too. If I wanted to *be* thrifty, I would cook large meals so I could live on leftovers for days, avoid buying takeaway coffees, and get the bus home from a night out rather than a taxi. Someone else aiming to be thrifty might decide on completely different thrifty behaviours.

In the same way that a business doesn't achieve its vision overnight, neither will you achieve your new 'be' goal straight away. Just because you spent thirty minutes learning how to code one day doesn't mean you have become a world-leading software programmer. Just because you smile at your daughter doesn't mean you've become a great parent. For 'be' goals to be fulfilled and new identities to be created, the behaviours need to be repeated over a sustained period. Time is the essential ingredient for your behaviours to assimilate into your identity. Your identity shapes your behaviours, but the reverse can also be true. If desired behaviours are maintained for long enough, then time will work its magic and create a new feature of your identity that aligns with those behaviours. Each time you behave in a way that is aligned with your desired future identity, your current identity is shaped a little more in that direction. This process allows us to fully use the motivational power of identity in creating our new lives.

If you are beginning a new healthy lifestyle, it's very unlikely that you will identify as *being* healthy. Most people want to become healthy because they are not currently healthy. It is more common to adopt a healthy new lifestyle because a doctor recommended it or your lover suggested your muffin top is excessive. These prods alone are insufficient motivation to sustain a healthy lifestyle in the long term, because the human mind doesn't rate these 'should' goals very highly. Any healthy behaviours you initiate will eventually be ditched. Instead, you want the healthy behaviours to be assimilated into your core identity, a process that motivation scientists call 'internalisation'.[160] Chapters three, four and five describe exactly how to maintain behaviours until your identity takes over the motivation responsibilities. A supportive motivational environment that provides opportunities to feel effective and valued also helps to sustain valued activities until identity takes control.

Put simply, until your new, desired identity and 'be' goals drive your behaviour, you have to *fake it till you make it*. If you have a desire to be a great son or daughter because you might not have been in the past, you might phone your mum every Saturday instead of avoiding making the call, for example. This will have a small but significant impact upon your identity. You are a step closer to viewing yourself as a great son or daughter. Every time you have a choice to make that involves being a great son/daughter or not, think about what someone who possesses this identity would do. After a while, your own identity will develop a 'wonderful son/daughter' component that makes behaviours that align with this identity a little more likely. Each action modifies your identity further and makes the next act a little easier. If the process is completed, the actions are fully assimilated into a new great son/daughter identity. Eventually, there is no need to think about what a great son or daughter would do, because you will have created your own identity to power your actions. Decisions that reflect your new identity take very little effort. Small, marginal steps over time accumulate into big lifestyle changes. Each decision to choose an act that signifies a great son/daughter makes the next choice a little bit easier, and momentum grows.

Social networks

It is not only your personal decisions and behaviours that influence your identity. In the words of Oscar Wilde:

> 'Most people are other people. Their thoughts are some-
> one else's opinions, their lives a mimicry, their passions a
> quotation.'

Your identity and your 'be' goals are significantly shaped by your social networks. If your three best friends are heavy drinkers, it's highly likely that you are a heavy drinker, too. If you hang around with hedonistic party animals, then you're probably a hedonistic party animal. Outliers exist – you might know a teetotaller who is close friends with a group of boozers – but this is an exception to the rule.

If formal and informal group memberships influence our identities, then they also shape our behaviour.[161] At university, my friends and I shared a collective identity largely based on lager and football, so a lot of what we did included these two things. It was part of who we were. But over the years, I spent less time with these friends. My social groups changed and so did my identity. I now rarely meet up with friends for the midday kick-off on TV and drink the cheapest four per cent lager all day. Having shared group identities helps build social bonds. If our closest friends value heavy metal music, then it pays for us to also value heavy metal music in order to fit in with the group.

Our social networks are so powerful that they even affect our genes. Many people still falsely believe that our genes cannot be modified. We cannot change what genes we inherit, but we can change whether certain genes are activated or not. An expression favoured by many scientists studying disease is: 'Our genes load the gun, but our environment pulls the trigger.' Our genes create an inclination towards developing a disease or not, but it's the environment that is the deciding factor for whether we are burdened by it. When our ancestors were alone, they were more likely to be attacked or have an accident. In these circumstances, the body needed to be ready to combat bacterial infection from cuts and wounds. As a result, genetic studies have shown that when people nowadays have poor social networks and feel isolated or lonely, the genes that control our response to bacterial infection are activated and relevant immune responses are readied. In contrast, in social groups, it was less likely that we'd be attacked or wounded, but much more likely that germs would spread. Hence, when we feel connected to social groups, the genes that control our response to *viral* infection are activated, and the body readies itself for combatting these viruses.

The social basis of identity is one of the reasons why some interventions aimed at getting people to be healthier work so well. Parkrun is a free community event where you can walk or run five kilometres around a public park. It's nothing short of a phenomenon in the UK and other parts of the world, with more than 1,100 events running every Saturday at 9am. One of the biggest reasons participants identify for doing Parkrun is a sense of collective identity and being part of a running community. Slimming World is equally inspiring because of its collective identity.[162] More than 19,000 weekly groups help 900,000 members across the UK and Republic of Ireland to lose weight and adjust their lifestyles collaboratively.

The power of our social networks can be used for developing new 'be' goals, but it can impede us too. You may be a complete novice at investing but want to *be*come a successful investor. If your existing social networks are not interested in investing, then they will offer little positive influence on your desired identity. This is not to say that you will fail, but you are not taking advantage of the power of a collective identity to support your 'be' goal. On the other hand, if you join an online investor community forum, then you suddenly throw yourself into a collection of people with investor identities who will shape yours too. This tactic will provide significant support to your goal of being a successful investor. This implicit support is complementary to the explicit support you will likely receive, such as encouragement and advice from the group of investors. Collective identity works in the same way for other 'be' goals. If you want to *be* an entrepreneur, hang out with entrepreneurs. If you want to *be* a musician, hang out with musicians.

In a nutshell

Your identity is a super motivator. It is one of the most powerful drivers of behaviour, even though most of the time you do not notice it working. Exercisers exercise, creatives create

and studious people study. 'Be' goals are the specific motivational component of identity that drives our behaviour. By
spending your well-earned time creating 'be' goals, it is possible to leverage the power of your identity to make changes
to your lifestyle and progress towards your ambitions, and to
live a fulfilling, mojo-packed life. 'Be' goals are underpinned
by mental processes that urge us to progress towards them
and correct behaviour if we do not. As a result, 'be' goals are
robust to obstacles, divert our attention away from failure
and require little effort to sustain. 'Be' goals are essential
if we want to be more like those lucky people who find life
effortless, who seem permanently motivated, engaged and in
control. They still go for a run despite the rain, they politely
decline the tempting pudding, and they never waste a day
bingeing on their favourite TV show. Time's potential to ruin
and disrupt dreams and ambitions recedes in people driven
by 'be' goals. Living in line with your 'be' goals and identity
will also drastically improve your mental health. Hamlet
never said the question was 'to have or not to have'. Who do
you want to *be*?

11

101 rules to master time*

'Time and space are modes by which we think and not conditions in which we live.'

– Albert Einstein, clever person

The aim of this book has been to describe and repair our broken relationship with time. Cultural developments in many parts of the world have conspired to shift our relationship with time from one of worship and reverence to one of ignorance and disrespect. We now treat time like a cheap, dispensable product, despite our relationship with time underpinning the entirety of our psychological and physical wellbeing.

I hope you have taken on plenty of tips, tricks and new ways of looking at your relationship with time to improve it for the better. By doing so, I'm confident that your mojo will improve, life will run a little smoother and your ambitions will be a little closer to being fulfilled. Even after reading this book, however, there may be periods in life when an enduring lack of time returns and the relationship fractures again. When this time comes, it would be careless of a book about

---

*   There are actually 117 rules, but 101 sounds better.

time to recommend reading the entire thing again. Instead, this chapter provides a menu of strategies described concisely without the underpinning rationale.

Across film and TV, you will find many absurd rules about how to master time. In the original *Terminator* film, it is only possible to travel back in time if you are naked. According to the rules in the *Back to the Future* movies, you'll pass out if you touch your past self. This final chapter provides over one hundred more practical directions that will enable you to repair your relationship with time. Some of this advice requires significant changes to the way you go about your life, while some just call for minor amendments that will provide incremental benefits. All will help you to re-energise your mojo. When you feel like time is your enemy, dip into this chapter and pick some tools from the box.

Chapter one

1.   Don't rely on your alarm clock if you can help it.
2.   If you live in China, live near Beijing. If you don't, live in the east of your time zone.
3.   Get some sunlight and exercise in the morning.
4.   Go to bed earlier on work-free days or stay in bed longer on workdays.

Chapter two

5.   Be more Violet Crawley. Busyness should not be a status symbol.
6.   Advocate for a four-day work week.

7. Don't think that feeling overly busy has anything to do with your schedule.

8. Don't speed while driving.

9. Seek work–life harmony, not work–life balance.

10. Don't presume your work–life harmony is the same as someone else's.

11. Uber-productivity or being 'on the go' is bad for your emotional health.

12. Adopt the Otto von Bismarck method to avoid time-wasters.

13. Turn off automatic notifications for emails and messages.

14. Only read emails and messages when you are prepared to give up your time for people.

15. Only read emails and messages when you have completed everything else you wanted to.

16. View emails as the lowest form of work activity that has ever existed.

17. Aim for inbox zero, not for a zero inbox.

18. Schedule work meetings to finish at least five or ten minutes before the next one.

19. Do not fill these post-meeting periods (see rule 18) with anything except finding some calm and balance.

20. Replace dead time with activities that are good for your mojo (see also rule 33).

21. If you're going to mindlessly scroll social media, combine it with stretching a body part that permanently hurts.

22. Have a reason for scrolling social media. Then stop.

23. Listen to something restorative on the work commute (see also rule 33).

24. Socially distance from family and friends who are overly busy.

25. Apply rule 24 to your online friends.

26. Tell loved ones you will be checking your phone a lot less from now on.

27. If you can't avoid overly busy friends, reduce the viral load by meeting them in a group environment.

28. Drastically reduce the length of your work meetings and other commitments.

29. When it's time to make a decision, give yourself ten minutes, not ten hours (but see rule 65 to make sure it's the right time to make a decision).

30. Diarise activities that help with your wellbeing, like breathing and periods of nothing.

31. Routinise as many things as possible, so you don't have to make any scheduling decisions.

32. Stretch the regularity of repetitive trivial tasks.

33. If you have some space in your diary after implementing the previous rules, feel free to add something that makes you feel competent, socially connected or like the captain of your own ship.

Chapter three

34. Willpower is designed to break. Do not rely on it.

35. Employing willpower will have negative implications for subsequent willpower. Do not rely on it.

36. Willpower is particularly fragile when you need it most. Do not rely on it.

37. If your resolve suddenly disappears, check for old lead pipes.

38. Replace 'don't' goals with 'do' goals that have a distinct end.

39. Do all activities that enhance your spirit as soon as possible in the day.

40. Be creative with your schedule to help with rule 39.

41. Make important decisions in the morning.

42. Put your alarm clock as far away from the bed as possible (but see rule 1).

43. Buy the most luxurious dressing gown and slippers you can afford.

44. Don't seek to emulate people who seem perfectionistic, obsessive or addicted.

Chapter four

45. Wars, recessions and other major events will derail your company's finances. Plan for this.

46. If someone wants to give you £10 now or £20 later, take the risk.

47. When developing projects, plan for how long your friend would take to complete it, not you.

48. Make Odysseus contracts to aid commitment. Pay for things in advance, arrange to meet your friend for a jog, tell everyone about your plans and ambitions, set up a regular savings amount.

49. Take a leaf out of Boris Johnson's playbook and peer into the future to see what you'll think and feel about your intentions.

Chapter five

50. Adopt the motivational perspective of children by doing things for the sake of doing them. Children know best.
51. If you can't apply rule 50, then seek a mental, social or any other immediate benefit for new activities.
52. Prioritise internal (often intangible) benefits over external (often tangible) benefits. The tangible benefits will follow in the long run.
53. Don't ruin people's existing motivation, especially children's, by adding an unnecessary incentive.
54. Start planning for when your prescription weight-loss drugs run out.
55. Make your actions and goals linguistically similar. Save money by modifying your finances rather than tightening your belt. Get healthy by eating healthy foods rather than going on a diet.
56. Be scientific and measure your actions and your progress towards goals. It's the only way you'll know what works.
57. Leverage the motivational power of enjoyable activities by linking them with not-so-enjoyable ones.
58. Choose one activity that will help you meet a goal or realise a dream.
59. Choose one outcome that will motivate your desired activity.

Chapter six

60. Have celebrations after the event, not before.

61. Keep the colonoscope in a little longer than necessary.
62. Do not tackle unimportant tasks just to get them off your to-do list.
63. Start tackling big tasks, even though it won't remove them from your to-do list.
64. Don't take the quick option at the expense of the good option.
65. Don't waste effort making a tricky decision now, when it's likely to turn into an easy decision later.
66. Don't trust the media in the lead-up to elections.
67. Remember the last four or five years when deciding who to vote for, not just the last year.
68. Save the best until last.
69. Don't let a negative end spoil a pleasant experience.
70. Don't let a positive end distract you from a negative experience.
71. Never pause the film at the scariest moment.
72. Beware the most expensive wine on the list.
73. If you have a job that includes difficult moments, spread them out.
74. Use 'red teams', colleagues and friends to negate your biases.
75. Always look for novelty among the mundane. Walk home a different way.
76. Use all your senses to help with rule 75.

Chapter seven

77. Set absurdly small goals at the beginning of an activity.
78. If rule 77 doesn't help, set even smaller goals.

79.   If rule 78 doesn't help, include preparatory tasks as goals.

80.   Establish the minimum effective effort. Do one set of exercises instead of three. Read the executive summary instead of the full report.

81.   Get things done early in the day to develop momentum.

82.   Avoid having a middle phase in activities and projects. The end of the beginning should be the beginning of the end.

83.   If applying rule 82 is impossible, incentivise and encourage (ideally with intrinsic motives) during the middle phases of a project.

84.   Don't get too stressed by the amount of work you still need to do. Your effort will increase near the end of a project.

85.   Don't undervalue windfalls and gifts.

86.   Don't be envious of others' talent.

87.   Define success as maximum effort, improvement and development. Winning is likely to follow.

88.   Don't define success by comparing yourself to others. Failure is likely to follow.

Chapter eight

89.   Seek regular solitude.

90.   If you feel anxious or lonely in solitude, suck it up.

91.   If you despise solitude, blame your parents.

92.   Don't fight boredom during solitude; it can be radical.

93.   Don't reach for your phone to rectify boredom; it will only increase it.

94.   Seek solitude in a place beyond your normal locations.

95. Turn off your phone during solitude.
96. If you want to run for solitude, run slowly.

Chapter nine

97. Don't rely on your memory to remember things accurately.
98. Be wary of psychology researchers messing with your memory. They'll make you remember drug-fuelled dogs and UFO abductions.
99. Delete your social media posts every now and then.
100. Parents – your support should be unconditional, but sometimes that support should be covert.
101. If your Japanese clients are silent, change your offer.
102. Try suffering in silence and letting time soothe your soul; you might be surprised.
103. Seek the support of others when times are *very* hard, not when they are hard.
104. Ensure that you have a social network to access when you *really* need it.
105. Make it very clear to your loved ones that you are there for them if *they* really need you.
106. Take on the responsibility of looking for signs that your loved ones might need you.

Chapter ten

107. Understand your identity by thinking about how you would label yourself.

108. Identify who you want to *be*.
109. Avoid doing things because you *should* do them.
110. Avoid the desire to *have* something.
111. Nouns are better than verbs when it comes to encouraging action.
112. If something goes wrong, blame the circumstances, not your character.
113. Create a varied identity; don't put all your eggs in one basket.
114. Adapt existing goals into 'be' goals; change 'starting a business' into 'being a successful businessperson'.
115. Identify the actions that express your desired identity.
116. Fake it till you make it.
117. Seek out social networks that match who you want to be.

Throughout the book, I've provided scientific or philosophical evidence for the effectiveness of these strategies. I can also vouch for many of these tactics because they helped me write this book. I often wrote a paragraph before I brushed my teeth in the morning (rule 39). I received immediate satisfaction from learning that Tom Hanks goes to a colonoscopy party, and many other fascinating discoveries (rule 51). During some evenings, I focused on opening the laptop, rather than being too ambitious and aiming to write any words (rules 77–79). These tactics meant I rarely had to dip into reserves of willpower (rules 34–36). Some of the best ideas developed during some time alone with my thoughts (rule 89). I've also discovered the mojo-enhancing benefits of turning my work emails off for days at a time (rule 16), switching my phone off (rule 95) and creating fictitious reasons to avoid needless meetings (rule 12). I sincerely hope you find some of these rules as effective as I did.

Acknowledgements

I would like to thank my agent, Andrew Gordon of David Higham Associates, who did agent things, took a punt on my idea and guided me expertly during book development. Thank you to the editorial team at Little, Brown, especially Holly Harley, whose turn of phrase in her feedback kept me entertained and on the right path throughout. Thanks to all my friends, especially Ben, Anthony and Kris, who encouraged me throughout with their enthusiastic requests for updates. Finally, the biggest thank you goes to my wonderful wife, Aimée, who continually juggled everything else so I could squeeze in some book-writing. I'm most eager to hear what she thinks about this book, which indicates that she means more to me than anyone else in the world.

Notes

Chapter one

1. Weiss, E. R., Todman, M., Maple, E., and Bunn, R. R. (2022). 'Boredom in a time of uncertainty: State and trait boredom's associations with psychological health during COVID-19'. *Behavioral Sciences*, 12(8), 298. https://doi.org/10.3390/bs12080298
2. van der Lippe, T. (2007). 'Dutch workers and time pressure: Household and workplace characteristics'. *Work, Employment and Society*, 21(4), 693–711. https://doi.org/10.1177/0950017007082877
3. Farmer, R., and Sundberg, N. D. (1986). 'Boredom proneness – the development and correlates of a new scale'. *Journal of Personality Assessment*, 50(1), 4–17. https://doi.org/10.1207/s15327752jpa5001_2
4. Abramson, E. E., and Stinson, S. G. (1977). 'Boredom and eating in obese and non-obese individuals'. *Addictive Behaviors*, 2(4), 181–185. https://doi.org/10.1016/0306-4603(77)90015-6
5. Kuerbis, A., Treloar Padovano, H., Shao, S., Houser, J., Muench, F. J., and Morgenstern, J. (2018). 'Comparing daily drivers of problem drinking among older and younger adults: An electronic daily diary study using smartphones'. *Drug and Alcohol Dependence*, 183, 240–246. https://doi.org/10.1016/j.drugalcdep.2017.11.012
6. Nederkoorn, C., Vancleef, L., Wilkenhöner, A., Claes, L., and Havermans, R. C. (2016). 'Self-inflicted pain out of boredom'. *Psychiatry Research*, 237, 127–132. https://doi.org/10.1016/j.psychres.2016.01.063
7. Zuzanek, J. (2004). 'Work, leisure, time pressure and stress'. In J. T. Haworth and A. J. Veal (eds), *Work and Leisure* (pp. 123–144). Routledge, New York.
8. Hoge, T. (2009). 'When work strain transcends psychological boundaries: An inquiry into the relationship between time pressure, irritation, work, family conflict and psychosomatic complaints'. *Stress and Health*, 25, 41–51.
9. Strazdins, L., Griffin, A. L., Broom, D. H., Banwell, C., Korda, R., Dixon, J., Paolucci, F., and Glover, J. (2011). 'Time scarcity: Another

health inequality?'. *Environment and Planning A: Economy and Space*, 43(3), 545–559. https://doi.org/10.1068/a4360

10. Naguy, A., Moodliar-Rensburg, S., and Alamiri, B. (2020). 'Coronaphobia and chronophobia – A psychiatric perspective'. *Asian Journal of Psychiatry*, 51, 102050. https://doi.org/10.1016/j.ajp.2020.102050

11. Information on the rates of anxiety and depression during the pandemic can be found here: https://www.apa.org/monitor/2021/11/numbers-depression-anxiety

12. Ogden, R. S. (2020). 'The passage of time during the UK COVID-19 lockdown'. *PLoS ONE*, 15(7), Article e0235871. https://doi.org/10.1371/journal.pone.0235871

13. Wittmann, M., Dinich, J., Merrow, M., and Roenneberg, T. (2006). 'Social jetlag: Misalignment of biological and social time'. *Chronobiology International*, 23(1–2), 497–509. https://doi.org/10.1080/07420520500545979

14. Caliandro, R., Streng, A. A., van Kerkhof, L. W. M., van der Horst, G. T. J., and Chaves, I. (2021). 'Social jetlag and related risks for human health: A timely review'. *Nutrients*, 13(12), 4543. https://doi.org/10.3390/nu13124543

15. Giuntella, O., and Mazzonna, F. (2019). 'Sunset time and the economic effects of social jetlag: Evidence from US time zone borders'. *Journal of Health Economics*, 65, 210–226. https://doi.org/10.1016/j.jhealeco.2019.03.007

16. Borisenkov, M. F., Tserne, T. A., Panev, A. S., Kuznetsova, E. S., Petrova, N. B., Timonin, V. D., ... Kasyanova, O. N. (2016). 'Seven-year survey of sleep timing in Russian children and adolescents: Chronic 1-h forward transition of social clock is associated with increased social jetlag and winter pattern of mood seasonality'. *Biological Rhythm Research*, 48(1), 3–12. https://doi.org/10.1080/09291016.2016.1223778

17. Roenneberg, T., Allebrandt, K. V., Merrow, M., and Vetter, C. (2012). 'Social jetlag and obesity'. *Current Biology: CB*, 22(10), 939–943.

18. Korman, M., Tkachev, V., Reis, C., Komada, Y., Kitamura, S., Gubin, D., Kumar, V., and Roenneberg, T. (2020). 'COVID-19-mandated social restrictions unveil the impact of social time pressure on sleep and body clock'. *Scientific Reports*, 10(1), 22225. https://doi.org/10.1038/s41598-020-79299-7

19. Blume, C., Garbazza, C., and Spitschan, M. (2019). 'Effects of light on human circadian rhythms, sleep and mood'. *Somnology: Sleep Research and Sleep Medicine*, 23(3), 147–156. https://doi.org/10.1007/s11818-019-00215-x

20. Shen, B., Ma, C., Wu, G., Liu, H., Chen, L., and Yang, G. (2023). 'Effects of exercise on circadian rhythms in humans'.

Frontiers in Pharmacology, 14, 1282357. https://doi.org/10.3389/
fphar.2023.1282357

Chapter two

21. Bellezza, S., Paharia, N., and Keinan, A. (2017). 'Conspicuous
consumption of time: When busyness and lack of leisure time
become a status symbol'. *Journal of Consumer Research*,
44(1), 118–138.
22. Details of the US and Irish four-day work week can be found here:
https://www.4dayweek.com/us-ireland-results
23. Details of the UK four-day work week can be found here: https://
autonomy.work/portfolio/uk4dwpilotresults/
24. Heesch, K. C., and Mâsse, L. C. (2004). 'Lack of time for physical
activity: Perception or reality for African American and Hispanic
women?'. *Women & Health*, 39(3), 45–62. https://doi.org/10.1300/
J013v39n03_04
25. The survey results about speeding can be found here: https://www.
brake.org.uk/get-involved/take-action/mybrake/knowledge-centre/
reports/lets-talk-about-speed-a-road-safety-week-survey-report
26. The average speed in London was taken from here: https://
www.tomtom.com/newsroom/explainers-and-insights/
london-is-the-worlds-slowest-city/
27. The survey can be found here: https://www.norc.org/research/
projects/gss.html
28. Gable, P. A., Wilhelm, A. L., and Poole, B. D. (2022). 'How does
emotion influence time perception? A review of evidence linking
emotional motivation and time processing'. *Frontiers in Psychology*,
13, 848154. https://doi.org/10.3389/fpsyg.2022.848154
29. Gable, P. A., and Poole, B. D. (2012). 'Time flies when you're having
approach-motivated fun: Effects of motivational intensity on time
perception'. *Psychological Science*, 23(8), 879–886. https://doi.org/
10.1177/0956797611435817
30. Grondin, S., Laflamme, V., and Gontier, É. (2014). 'Effect on
perceived duration and sensitivity to time when observing disgusted
faces and disgusting mutilation pictures'. *Attention, Perception, &
Psychophysics*, 76, 1522–1534. doi:10.3758/s13414-014-0682-7
31. Campbell, L. A., and Bryant, R. A. (2007). 'How time flies: A
study of novice skydivers'. *Behaviour Research and Therapy*, 45(6),
1389–1392. https://doi.org/10.1016/j.brat.2006.05.011
32. Burrage, E., Marshall, K. L., Santanam, N., and Chantler, P. D.
(2018). 'Cerebrovascular dysfunction with stress and depression'.
Brain Circulation, 4(2), 43–53. https://doi.org/10.4103/bc.bc_6_18

33. Soares, J. M., Sampaio, A., Ferreira, L. M., Santos, N. C., Marques, F., Palha, J. A., Cerqueira, J. J., and Sousa, N. (2012). 'Stress-induced changes in human decision-making are reversible'. *Translational Psychiatry* 2(7): e131, doi:10.1038/tp.2012.59.

34. Renaud K., Ramsay J., and Hair M. (2006). '"You've got e-mail!"... shall I deal with it now? Electronic mail from the recipient's perspective'. *International Journal of Human-Computer Interaction.* 21:313–332. doi: 10.1207/s15327590ijhc2103_3.

35. Sadeghi, S., Takeuchi, H., Shalani, B., Taki, Y., Nouchi, R., Yokoyama, R., Kotozaki, Y., Nakagawa, S., Sekiguchi, A., Iizuka, K., Hanawa, S., Araki, T., Miyauchi, C. M., Sakaki, K., Nozawa, T., Ikeda, S., Yokota, S., Magistro, D., Sassa, Y., and Kawashima, R. (2022). 'Brain anatomy alterations and mental health challenges correlate to email addiction tendency'. *Brain Sciences*, 12(10), 1278. https://doi.org/10.3390/brainsci12101278

36. Scherer, K. R. (2003). 'Vocal communication of emotion: A review of research paradigms'. *Speech Communication*, 40 (1–2), 227–256.

37. Rueff-Lopes, R., Navarro, J., Caetano, A., and Junça Silva, A. (2015). 'A Markov chain analysis of emotional exchange in voice-to-voice communication: Testing for the mimicry hypothesis of emotional contagion'. *Human Communication Research*, 41, 412–434.

38. Kramer, A. D. I., Guillory, J. E., and Hancock, J. T. (2014). 'Experimental evidence of massive-scale emotional contagion through social networks'. *Proceedings of the National Academy of Sciences of the United States of America*, 111(24), 8788–8790. https://doi.org/10.1073/pnas.1320040111

39. Ryan, R. M., and Deci, E. L. (2017). 'Self-determination theory: Basic psychological needs in motivation, development, and wellness'. *The Guilford Press*. https://doi.org/10.1521/978.14625/28806

Chapter three

40. Duckworth, A. L., and Kern, M. L. (2011). 'A meta analysis of the convergent validity of self control measures'. *Journal of Research in Personality*, 45(3), 259–268. https://doi.org/10.1016/j.jrp.2011.02.004

41. A great book on this idea is *Too Much of a Good Thing* by Lee Goldman (published by Hachette).

42. Shultz, S., Opie, C., and Atkinson, Q. D. (2011). 'Stepwise evolution of stable sociality in primates'. *Nature*, 479(7372), 219–222. https://doi.org/10.1038/nature10601

43. Dunbar, R. I. M. (2003). 'The social brain: Mind, language, and society in evolutionary perspective'. *Annual Review of*

Anthropology, 32, 163–181. https://doi.org/10.1146/annurev. anthro.32.061002.093158

44. Passingham, R. E., 'Evolution of the prefrontal cortex in the hominins'. In *Understanding the Prefrontal Cortex: Selective advantage, connectivity, and neural operations*, Oxford Psychology Series (Oxford, 2021; online edn, Oxford Academic, 19 Aug. 2021), https://doi.org/10.1093/oso/9780198844570.003.0009

45. Saunders, B., and Inzlicht, M. (2016). 'Vigour and fatigue: How variation in affect underlies effective self-control'. In T. S. Braver (ed.), *Motivation and Cognitive Control* (pp. 211–234). Routledge/Taylor & Francis Group.

46. Inzlicht, M., and Legault, L. (2014). 'No pain, no gain: How distress underlies effective self-control (and unites diverse social psychological phenomena)'. In J. P. Forgas and E. Harmon-Jones eds), *Motivation and its Regulation: The Control Within* (pp. 115–132). Psychology Press.

47. Baumeister, R. F., Bratslavsky, E., Muraven, M., and Tice, D. M. (1998). 'Ego depletion: Is the active self a limited resource?'. *Journal of Personality and Social Psychology*, 74(5), 1252–1265. https://doi. org/10.1037/0022-3514.74.5.1252

48. Boat, R., and Taylor, I. M. (2017). 'Prior self-control exertion and perceptions of pain during a physically demanding task'. *Psychology of Sport and Exercise*, 33, 1–6. https://doi.org/10.1016/ j.psychsport.2017.07.005

49. Milyavskaya, M., and Inzlicht, M. (2018). 'Attentional and motivational mechanisms of self-control'. In D. de Ridder, M. Adriaanse, and K. Fujita (eds), *The Routledge International Handbook of Self-Control in Health and Wellbeing* (pp. 11–23). Routledge/Taylor & Francis Group. https://doi.org/10.4324/ 9781315648576-2

50. Arnsten, A., Mazure, C. M., and Sinha, R. (2012). 'This is your brain in meltdown'. *Scientific American*, 306(4), 48–53. https://doi.org/ 10.1038/scientificamerican0412-48

51. Oscarsson, M., Carlbring, P., Andersson, G., and Rozental, A. (2020). 'A large-scale experiment on New Year's resolutions: Approach-oriented goals are more successful than avoidance-oriented goals'. *PLoS ONE*, 15(12), Article e0234097. https://doi.org/10.1371/ journal.pone.0234097

52. Leone, M. J., Fernandez Slezak, D., Golombek, D., and Sigman, M. (2017). 'Time to decide: Diurnal variations on the speed and quality of human decisions'. *Cognition*, 158, 44–55. https://doi.org/10.1016/ j.cognition.2016.10.007

53. Details of the Italian chronotype study were taken from here: https://medicalxpress.com/news/2021-05-night-owl-odds-diabetes-youre.html

54. Details of the Finnish chronotype study were taken from here: https://www.bmj.com/company/newsroom/night-owls-may-be-twice-as-likely-as-morning-larks-to-underperform-at-work/

Chapter four

55. Chance, Z., Norton, M. I., Gino, F., and Ariely, D. (2011). 'Temporal view of the costs and benefits of self-deception'. *Proceedings of the National Academy of Sciences of the United States of America*, 108(Suppl 3), 15655–15659. https://doi.org/10.1073/pnas.1010658108
56. Adler, H. M., and Larson, J. A. (1928). 'Deception and self-deception'. *Journal of Abnormal and Social Psychology*, 22(4), 364–371. https://doi.org/10.1037/h0076012
57. Lee, B. (2017). *The Dangerous Case of Donald Trump: 27 Psychiatrists and Mental Health Experts Assess a President*. New York: Thomas Dunne Books.
58. Read, D., and van Leeuwen, B. (1998). 'Predicting hunger: The effects of appetite and delay on choice'. *Organizational Behavior and Human Decision Processes*, 76(2), 189–205. https://doi.org/10.1006/obhd.1998.2803
59. Read, D., Loewenstein, G., and Kalyanaraman, S. (1999). 'Mixing virtue and vice: Combining the immediacy effect and the diversification heuristic'. *Journal of Behavioral Decision Making*, 12(4), 257–273. https://doi.org/10.1002/(SICI)1099-0771(199912)12:4<257::AID-BDM327>3.0.CO;2-6
60. Data on the likelihood of pandemic was found here: https://globalhealth.duke.edu/news/statistics-say-large-pandemics-are-more-likely-we-thought
61. Data on the likelihood of recession was found here: https://www.kiplinger.com/slideshow/investing/t038-s001-recessions-10-facts-you-must-know/index.html#:~:text=Again%2C%20since%201857%2C%20a%20recession,and%2Da%2Dquarter%20years.
62. Ericson, K. M., White, J. M., Laibson, D., and Cohen, J. D. (2015). 'Money earlier or later? Simple heuristics explain intertemporal choices better than delay discounting does'. *Psychological Science*, 26(6), 826–833. https://doi.org/10.1177/0956797615572232
63. Ludwig, R. M., Flournoy, J. C., and Berkman, E. T. (2019). 'Inequality in personality and temporal discounting across socioeconomic status? Assessing the evidence'. *Journal of Research in Personality*, 81, 79–87. https://doi.org/10.1016/j.jrp.2019.05.003

Chapter five

64. Simone D'Ambrogio, S., Werksman, N., Platt, M. L., and Johnson, E. N. (2022). 'How celebrity status and gaze direction in ads drive visual attention to shape consumer decisions'. *Psychology & Marketing*, 40, 723–734. https://doi.org/10.1002/mar.21772

65. This paper provides a great overview of the science behind the whole chapter: Kruglanski, A. W., Fishbach, A., Woolley, K., Bélanger, J. J., Chernikova, M., Molinario, E., and Pierro, A. (2018). 'A structural model of intrinsic motivation: On the psychology of means-ends fusion'. *Psychological Review*, 125(2), 165–182. https://doi.org/10.1037/rev0000095

66. Woolley, K., and Fishbach, A. (2018). 'It's about time: Earlier rewards increase intrinsic motivation'. *Journal of Personality and Social Psychology*, 114(6), 877–890. https://doi.org/10.1037/pspa0000116

67. Deci, E. L., Koestner, R., and Ryan, R. M. (1999). 'A meta-analytic review of experiments examining the effects of extrinsic rewards on intrinsic motivation'. *Psychological Bulletin*, 125(6), 627–668. https://doi.org/10.1037/0033-2909.125.6.627

68. Maimaran, M., and Fishbach, A. (2014). 'If it's useful and you know it, do you eat? Preschoolers refrain from instrumental food'. *Journal of Consumer Research*, 41(3), 642–655. https://doi.org/10.1086/677224

69. Information on medicalising obesity can be found here: https://journalofethics.ama-assn.org/article/medicalizing-obesity-individual-economic-and-medical-consequences/2011-12

70. Faster runners run slower: Emig, T., Peltonen, J. (2020). 'Human running performance from real-world big data'. *Nature Communications*, 11, 4936. https://doi.org/10.1038/s41467-020-18737-6

71. Sansone, C., Sachau, D. A., and Weir, C. (1989). 'Effects of instruction on intrinsic interest: The importance of context'. *Journal of Personality and Social Psychology*, 57(5), 819–829.

72. Wolfe, J. B. (1936). 'Effectiveness of token rewards for chimpanzees'. *Comparative Psychological Monographs*, 12, 1–72.

73. Bélanger, J. J., Schori-Eyal, N., Pica, G., Kruglanski, A. W., and Lafrenière, M.-A. (2015). 'The "more is less" effect in equifinal structures: Alternative means reduce the intensity and quality of motivation'. *Journal of Experimental Social Psychology*, 60, 93–102. https://doi.org/10.1016/j.jesp.2015.05.005

Chapter six

74. Redelmeier, D. A., and Kahneman, D. (1996). 'Patients' memories of painful medical treatments: Real-time and retrospective evaluations of two minimally invasive procedures'. *Pain*, 66(1), 3–8. https://doi.org/10.1016/0304-3959(96)02994-6

75. Kahneman, D., Fredrickson, B. L., Schreiber, C. A., and Redelmeier, D. A. (1993). 'When more pain is preferred to less: Adding a better end'. *Psychological Science*, 4(6), 401–405. https://doi.org/10.1111/j.1467-9280.1993.tb00589.x

76. Roberts, A. R., Imas, A., and Fishbach, A. (2023). 'Can't wait to pay: The desire for goal closure increases impatience for costs'. *Journal of Personality and Social Psychology*. Advance online publication. https://doi.org/10.1037/pspa0000367

77. Rosenbaum, D. A., Gong, L., and Potts, C. A. (2014). 'Pre-crastination: Hastening subgoal completion at the expense of extra physical effort'. *Psychological Science*, 25(7), 1487–1496. https://doi.org/10.1177/0956797614532657

78. Wasserman, E. A., and Brzykcy S. J. (2015). 'Pre-crastination in the pigeon'. *Psychonomic Bulletin & Review*, 22, 1130–1134.

79. Lenz, G. S. (2013). 'Substituting the end for the whole: Why voters respond primarily to the election year economy'. *American Journal of Political Science*, 58, 31–47. https://doi.org/10.1111/ajps.12053

80. Bortels, L. (2008). 'Economics still matters to poorer voters'. *Challenge*, 51(6), 38–51. https://www.jstor.org/stable/40722545

81. Gavin, Neil T., and David Sanders. (1997). 'The economy and voting'. *Parliamentary Affairs*, 50(4), 631. Gale Academic OneFile, link.gale.com/apps/doc/A363688621/AONE?u=anon~866b8b4a&sid=googleScholar&xid=3f7c0c9a. Accessed 30 May 2024.

82. Tversky, A., and Kahneman, D. (1973). 'Availability: A heuristic for judging frequency and probability'. *Cognitive Psychology*, 5(2), 207–232. https://doi.org/10.1016/0010-0285(73)90033-9

83. Do, A. M., Rupert, A. V., and Wolford, G. (2008). 'Evaluations of pleasurable experiences: The peak-end rule'. *Psychonomic Bulletin & Review*, 15(1), 96–98. https://doi.org/10.3758/PBR.15.1.96

84. Müller, U. W. D., Witteman, C. L. M., Spijker, J., and Alpers, G. W. (2019). 'All's bad that ends bad: There is a peak end memory bias in anxiety'. *Frontiers in Psychology*, 10, 1272. https://doi.org/10.3389/fpsyg.2019.01272

85. Alaybek, B., Dalal, R. S., Fyffe, S., Aitken, J. A., Zhou, Y., Qu, X., Roman, A., and Baines, J. I. (2022). 'All's well that ends (and peaks) well? A meta-analysis of the peak-end rule and duration neglect'. *Organizational Behavior and Human Decision Processes*, 170, Article 104149. https://doi.org/10.1016/j.obhdp.2022.104149

86. Hutchinson, J. C., Zenko, Z., Santich, S., and Dalton, P. C. (2020). 'Increasing the pleasure and enjoyment of exercise: A novel resistance-training protocol'. *Journal of Sport & Exercise Psychology*, 42(2), 143–152. https://doi.org/10.1123/jsep.2019-0089

87. Hoogerheide, V., Vink, M., Finn, B., Raes, A. K., and Paas, F. (2018). 'How to bring the news … peak-end effects in children's affective responses to peer assessments of their social behavior'. *Cognition and Emotion*, 32(5), 1114–1121. https://doi.org/10.1080/02699931.2017.1362375

88. De Maeyer, P., and Estelami, H. (2013). 'Applying the peak-end rule to reference prices'. *Journal of Product & Brand Management*, 22(3), 260–265. https://doi.org/10.1108/JPBM-04-2013-0290

89. Kang, P., Daniels, D. P., and Schweitzer, M. E. (2022). 'The streak-end rule: How past experiences shape decisions about future behaviors in a large-scale natural field experiment with volunteer crisis counselors'. *Proceedings of the National Academy of Sciences of the United States of America*, 119(45), e2204460119. https://doi.org/10.1073/pnas.2204460119

90. Bagheri, L., and Milyavskaya, M. (2019). 'Novelty–variety as a candidate basic psychological need: New evidence across three studies'. *Motivation and Emotion*, 44, 32–53. https://link.springer.com/article/10.1007/s11031-019-09807-4

91. Shohamy, D., and Adcock, R. A. (2010). 'Dopamine and adaptive memory'. *Trends in Cognitive Sciences*, 14(10), 464–472. https://doi.org/10.1016/j.tics.2010.08.002

92. Ramaswami M. (2014). 'Network plasticity in adaptive filtering and behavioral habituation'. *Neuron*, 82(6), 1216–1229. https://doi.org/10.1016/j.neuron.2014.04.035

93. Matthews W. J. (2011). 'Stimulus repetition and the perception of time: The effects of prior exposure on temporal discrimination, judgment, and production'. *PLoS ONE*, 6(5), e19815. https://doi.org/10.1371/journal.pone.0019815

94. Novelty and mindfulness: Langer, E. J., and M. Moldoveanu (2000). 'The construct of mindfulness'. *Journal of Social Issues*, 56(1), 1–9.

Chapter seven

95. Kurzban, R., Duckworth, A., Kable, J. W., and Myers, J. (2013). 'An opportunity cost model of subjective effort and task performance'. *Behavioral and Brain Sciences*, 36(6), 661–679. https://doi.org/10.1017/S0140525X12003196

96. Ferguson, C., Langwith, C., Muldoon, A., and Leonard, J. (2010). *Improving Obesity Management in Adult Primary Care*. Washington, DC: George Washington University.

97. Histed, M. H., Pasupathy, A., and Miller, E. K. (2009). 'Learning substrates in the primate prefrontal cortex and striatum: Sustained activity related to successful actions'. *Neuron*, 63(2), 244–253. https://doi.org/10.1016/j.neuron.2009.06.019

98. Todd, J. S., Shurley, J. P., and Todd, T. C. (2012). 'Thomas L. DeLorme and the science of progressive resistance exercise'. *Journal of Strength and Conditioning Research*, 26(11), 2913–2923. https://doi.org/10.1519/JSC.0b013e31825adcb4

99. Ian McQueen's thesis on the number of repetitions can be found here: https://core.ac.uk/download/77018594.pdf

100. Info on Arthur Jones's experiment can be found here: http://arthurjonesexercise.com/Athletic/Colorado.PDF

101. Atkinson, G., Peacock, O., St Clair Gibson, A., and Tucker, R. (2007). 'Distribution of power output during cycling: impact and mechanisms'. *Sports Medicine* (Auckland, N.Z.), 37(8), 647–667. https://doi.org/10.2165/00007256-200737080-00001

102. Webb, O. J., and Cotton, D. R. E. (2019). 'Deciphering the sophomore slump: Changes to student perceptions during the undergraduate journey'. *Higher Education*, 77. DOI:10.1007/s10734-018-0268-8

103. Deci, E. L., Olafsen, A. H., and Ryan, R. M. (2017). 'Self-determination theory in work organizations: The state of a science'. *Annual Review of Organizational Psychology and Organizational Behavior*, 4, 19–43. https://doi.org/10.1146/annurev-orgpsych-032516-113108

104. A scientific article that is relevant here and covers other elements of this chapter: Inzlicht, M., Shenhav, A., and Olivola, C. Y. (2018). 'The effort paradox: Effort is both costly and valued'. *Trends in Cognitive Sciences*, 22(4), 337–349. https://doi.org/10.1016/j.tics.2018.01.007

105. Norton, M. I., Mochon, D., and Ariely, D. (2012). 'The IKEA effect: When labor leads to love'. *Journal of Consumer Psychology*, 22(3), 453–460. https://doi.org/10.1016/j.jcps.2011.08.002

106. Arkes, H. R., Joyner, C. A., Pezzo, M. V., Nash, J. G., Siegel-Jacobs, K., and Stone, E. (1994). 'The psychology of windfall gains'. *Organizational Behavior and Human Decision Processes*, 59(3), 331–347. https://doi.org/10.1006/obhd.1994.1063

107. Muehlbacher, S., and Kirchler, E. (2009). 'Origin of endowments in public good games: The impact of effort on contributions'. *Journal of Neuroscience, Psychology and Economics*, 2, 59–67.

108. London Marathon Statistics were taken from here: https://www.independent.co.uk/sport/general/athletics/london-marathon-2024-record-number-participants-b2532782.html

109. Aronson, E., and Mills, J. (1959). 'The effect of severity of initiation on liking for a group'. *Journal of Abnormal and Social Psychology*. 59, 177–181.

110. The story of Mozart and info on the Milano study was based on this online article: https://www.psychologytoday.com/us/blog/one-among-many/202105/mozart-and-the-effort-paradox#:~:text=The%20 connection%20between%20effort%20and,et%20al.%2C%202018

111. Nicholls, J. G. (1984). 'Achievement motivation: Conceptions of ability, subjective experience, task choice, and performance'. *Psychological Review*, 91(3), 328–346. https://doi.org/10.1037/ 0033-295X.91.3.328

112. Duda, J., and Hall, H. (2001). 'Achievement goal theory in sport: Recent extensions and future directions'. In R. Singer, H. Hausenblas, and C. Janelle (eds), *Handbook of Sport Psychology* (2nd edn, pp. 417–443). John Wiley and Sons.

Chapter eight

113. Suedfeld, P., Ramirez, C., Deaton, J., and Baker-Brown, G. (1982). 'Reactions and attributes of prisoners in solitary confinement'. *Criminal Justice and Behavior*, 9(3), 303–340. https://doi.org/ 10.1177/0093854882009003004

114. The letter from Nelson to Winnie Mandela can be found here: https://www.panmacmillan.com/blogs/general/ a-letter-from-nelson-mandela-to-winnie-mandela.

115. Long, C. R., and Averill, J. R. (2003). 'Solitude: An exploration of benefits of being alone'. *Journal for the Theory of Social Behaviour*, 33(1), 21–44. https://doi.org/10.1111/1468-5914.00204

116. Pfeifer, E., Geyer, N., Storch, F., and Wittmann, M. (2019). '"Just Think": Students feel significantly more relaxed, less aroused, and in a better mood after a period of silence alone in a room'. *Psych*, 1(1), 343–352. https://doi.org/10.3390/psych1010024

117. Kuwabara, T., Naruiwa, N., Kawabe, T., Kato, N., Sasaki, A., Ikeda, A., Otani, S., Imura, S., Watanabe, K., and Ohno, G. (2021). 'Human change and adaptation in Antarctica: Psychological research on Antarctic wintering-over at Syowa station'. *International Journal of Circumpolar Health*, 80(1), 1886704. https://doi.org/10.1080/ 22423982.2021.1886704

118. Wilson, T. D., Reinhard, D. A., Westgate, E. C., Gilbert, D. T., Ellerbeck, N., Hahn, C., Brown, C. L., and Shaked, A. (2014). 'Just think: the challenges of the disengaged mind'. *Science*, 345(6192), 75–77. https://doi.org/10.1126/science.1250830

119. Information on the ineffectiveness of video doorbells was found here: https://www.scientificamerican.com/article/do-video-doorbells-really-prevent-crime/#:~:text=%E2%80%9CThe%20risks%20of%20being%20 caught,pretty%20substantial%2C%E2%80%9D%20noted%20Stickle

120. The story about stealing a tank was found here: https://www.bbc. co.uk/news/blogs-news-from-elsewhere-42634753

121. Details on the survey can be found here: https://www.bhf.org.uk/ what-we-do/news-from-the-bhf/news-archive/2018/september/ the-average-brit-spends-five-years-of-their-life-feeling-bored

122. Chin, A., Markey, A., Bhargava, S., Kassam, K. S., and Loewenstein, G. (2017). 'Bored in the USA: Experience sampling and boredom in everyday life'. *Emotion,* 17(2), 359–368. https://doi.org/10.1037/ emo0000232

123. Information on boredom across the lifespan was found here: https:// www.bps.org.uk/psychologist/boredom-across-lifespan

124. van Tilburg, W. A. P., Igou, E. R., and Panjwani, M. (2023). 'Boring people: Stereotype characteristics, interpersonal attributions, and social reactions'. *Personality and Social Psychology Bulletin*, 49(9), 1329–1343. https://doi.org/10.1177/01461672221079104

125. Britton, A., and Shipley, M. J. (2010). 'Bored to death?'. *International Journal of Epidemiology*, 39(2), 370–371. https://doi.org/10.1093/ ije/dyp404

126. Pfattheicher, S., Lazarević, L. B., Westgate, E. C., and Schindler, S. (2021). 'On the relation of boredom and sadistic aggression'. *Journal of Personality and Social Psychology*, 121(3), 573–600. https://doi. org/10.1037/pspi0000335

127. Tam, K. Y. Y., and Inzlicht, M. (2024). 'Fast-forward to boredom: How switching behavior on digital media makes people more bored'. *Journal of Experimental Psychology*: *General,* 153(10), 2409–2426. Advance online publication. https://doi.org/10.1037/xge0001639

128. Pfeifer, E., and Wittmann, M. (2020). 'Waiting, thinking, and feeling: Variations in the perception of time during silence'. *Frontiers in Psychology*, 11, 602. https://doi.org/10.3389/fpsyg.2020.00602

Chapter nine

129. Details of Malcolm Alexander's case were taken from here: https:// innocenceproject.org/cases/malcolm-alexander/

130. Statistics on eyewitness misidentification were taken from here: https://innocenceproject.org/eyewitness-misidentification/

131. Sivers, H., Schooler, J., Freyd, J. J. (2002). 'Recovered memories'. In V.S. Ramachandran (ed.) *Encyclopedia of the Human Brain, Volume 4* (pp. 169–184). San Diego, California and London: Academic Press.

132. Magnussen, S., Andersson, J., Cornoldi, C., De Beni, R., Endestad, T., Goodman, G. S., Helstrup, T., Koriat, A., Larsson, M., Melinder, A., Nilsson, L. G., Rönnberg, J., and Zimmer, H. (2006). 'What

people believe about memory'. *Memory*, 14(5), 595–613. https://doi.
org/https://doi.org/10.1080/09658210600646716

133. Patihis, L., Ho, L. Y., Tingen, I. W., Lilienfeld, S. O., and Loftus, E.
F. (2014). 'Are the "memory wars" over? A scientist practitioner gap
in beliefs about memory'. *Psychological Science*, 25(2), 519–530.
https://doi.org/https://doi.org/10.1177/0956797613510718

134. Braun, K. A., Ellis, R., and Loftus, E. F. (2002). 'Make my memory:
How advertising can change our memories of the past'. *Psychology &
Marketing*, 19(1), 1–23. https://doi.org/10.1002/mar.1000

135. Berkowitz, S. R., Laney, C., Morris, E. K., Garry, M., and Loftus, E.
F. (2008). 'Pluto behaving badly: False beliefs and their consequences'.
American Journal of Psychology, 121(4), 643–660.

136. Otgaar, H., Candel, I., Merckelbach, H., and Wade, K.A. (2009).
'Abducted by a UFO: Prevalence information affects young children's
false memories for an implausible event'. *Applied Cognitive
Psychology*, 23, 115–125.

137. Otgaar, H., Candel, I., and Merckelbach, H. (2008). 'Children's
false memories: Easier to elicit for a negative than for a neutral
event'. *Acta Psychologica*, 128(2), 350–354. https://doi.org/10.1016/
j.actpsy.2008.03.009

138. Roediger, H. L., and McDermott, K.B. (1995). 'Creating false
memories: Remembering words not presented in lists'. *Journal of
Experimental Psychology: Learning, Memory, and Cognition*,
21, 803–814.

139. Blumen, H. M., and Rajaram, S. (2008). 'Influence of re-exposure
and retrieval disruption during group collaboration on later
individual recall'. *Memory*, 16(3), 231–244. https://doi.org/10.1080/
09658210701804495

140. Jackson, M. (2004). 'The prose of suffering and the practice of
silence'. *Spiritus* 4, 44–59. https://doi.org/10.1353/scs.2004.011.

141. Krause N. (2010). 'Assessing coping responses within specific faith
traditions: Suffering in silence, stress, and depressive symptoms
among older catholics'. *Mental Health, Religion & Culture*, 13(5),
513–529. https://doi.org/10.1080/13674670903433686

142. Krause N. (2010). 'Receiving social support at church when stressful
life events arise: Do catholics and protestants differ?'. *Psychology
of Religion and Spirituality*, 2(4), 234–246. https://doi.org/
10.1037/a0020036

143. Krause N., and Bastida E. (2009). 'Religion, suffering, and health
among older Mexican Americans'. *Journal of Aging Studies*,
23:114–123.

144. Krause, N. (1997). 'Received support, anticipated support, social
class, and mortality'. *Research on Aging*, 19(4), 387–422. https://doi.
org/10.1177/0164027597194001

Chapter ten

145. Juster, R. P., Smith, N. G., Ouellet, É., Sindi, S., and Lupien, S. J. (2013). 'Sexual orientation and disclosure in relation to psychiatric symptoms, diurnal cortisol, and allostatic load'. *Psychosomatic Medicine*, 75(2), 103–116. https://doi.org/10.1097/PSY.0b013e3182826881

146. McGarrity, L. A., and Huebner, D. M. (2014). 'Is being out about sexual orientation uniformly healthy? The moderating role of socioeconomic status in a prospective study of gay and bisexual men'. *Annals of Behavioral Medicine*, 47(1), 28–38. https://doi.org/10.1007/s12160-013-9575-6

147. Pachankis, J. E., Mahon, C. P., Jackson, S. D., Fetzner, B. K., and Bränström, R. (2020). 'Sexual orientation concealment and mental health: A conceptual and meta-analytic review'. *Psychological Bulletin*, 146(10), 831–871. https://doi.org/10.1037/bul0000271

148. Brownfield, J. M., Brown, C., Jeevanba, S. B., and VanMattson, S. B. (2018). 'More than simply getting bi: An examination of coming out growth for bisexual individuals'. *Psychology of Sexual Orientation and Gender Diversity*, 5(2), 220–232. https://doi.org/10.1037/sgd0000282

149. Interview with Kaetlyn Osmond on athletic retirement can be found here: https://www.cbc.ca/sports/olympics/winter/figure-skating/kaetlyn-osmond-figure-skating-retirement-scott-russell-1.5119954

150. Voorheis, P., Silver, M., and Consonni, J. (2023). 'Adaptation to life after sport for retired athletes: A scoping review of existing reviews and programs'. *PLoS ONE*, 18(9), Article e0291683. https://doi.org/10.1371/journal.pone.0291683

151. D'Argembeau A. (2013). 'On the role of the ventromedial prefrontal cortex in self-processing: the valuation hypothesis'. *Frontiers in Human Neuroscience*, 7, 372. https://doi.org/10.3389/fnhum.2013.00372

152. Carver, C. S., and Scheier, M. F. (1998). *On the Self-Regulation of Behavior*. Cambridge University Press. https://doi.org/10.1017/CBO9781139174794

153. Berkman, E. T., Livingston, J. L., and Kahn, L. E. (2017). 'Finding the "self" in self-regulation: The identity-value model'. *Psychological Inquiry*, 28(2–3), 77–98. https://doi.org/10.1080/1047840X.2017.1323463

154. Harmon-Jones, E., and Mills, J. (2019). 'An introduction to cognitive dissonance theory and an overview of current perspectives on the theory'. In E. Harmon-Jones (ed.), *Cognitive Dissonance: Re-examining a Pivotal Theory in Psychology* (2nd edn, pp. 3–24). American Psychological Association. https://doi.org/10.1037/0000135-001

155. Bryan, C. J., Master, A., and Walton, G. M. (2014). '"Helping" versus "being a helper": Invoking the self to increase helping in young children'. *Child Development*, 85(5), 1836–1842. https://doi.org/10.1111/cdev.12244

156. Miller, R. L., Brickman, P., and Bolen, D. (1975). 'Attribution versus persuasion as a means for modifying behavior'. *Journal of Personality and Social Psychology*, 31(3), 430–441. https://doi.org/10.1037/h0076539

157. Burger, J. M., and Caldwell, D. F. (2003). 'The effects of monetary incentives and labeling on the foot-in-the-door effect: Evidence for a self-perception process'. *Basic and Applied Social Psychology*, 25(3), 235–241. https://doi.org/10.1207/S15324834BASP2503_06

158. Bryan, C. J., Adams, G. S., and Monin, B. (2013). 'When cheating would make you a cheater: Implicating the self prevents unethical behavior'. *Journal of Experimental Psychology: General*, 142(4), 1001–1005. https://doi.org/10.1037/a0030655

159. Bryan, C. J., Walton, G. M., Rogers, T., and Dweck, C. S. (2011). 'Motivating voter turnout by invoking the self'. *Proceedings of the National Academy of Sciences of the United States of America*, 108(31), 12653–12656. https://doi.org/10.1073/pnas.1103343108

160. Deci, E. L., and Ryan, R. M. (2000). 'The "what" and "why" of goal pursuits: Human needs and the self-determination of behavior'. *Psychological Inquiry*, 11(4), 227–268. https://doi.org/10.1207/S15327965PLI1104_01

161. Brewer, M. B., and Hewstone, M. (eds). (2004). *Self and Social Identity*. Blackwell Publishing.

162. Warhurst, R., and Black, K. (2021). 'Lost and found: Parkrun, work and identity'. *Qualitative Research in Sport, Exercise and Health*, 14(3), 397–412. https://doi.org/10.1080/2159676X.2021.1924244

Index